Heath United Methodist Church

W. Richard Weddle, Pastor

1149 Hebron Rd., Heath, Ohio 43056   Church 522-3155   Res. 522 1719

Presented by:

REV. ARNOLD ETTENHOFER

HURDLES TO HEAVEN

HURDLES
TO
HEAVEN

by Brian Whitlow

Harper & Row, Publishers, New York and Evanston

To the Most Reverend Harold E. Sexton, Archbishop of British Columbia, under whom I have had the honor of serving for eight very happy years.

CONTENTS

ACKNOWLEDGMENTS

Acknowledgment for permission to quote is due to the Society for the Propagation of Christian Knowledge for a prayer composed by Frank Bennett; to the Very Rev. Eric Milner-White, Dean of York, for a prayer from his *Cambridge Bede Book;* to the Harold Matson Company of New York for permission to quote from *The Caine Mutiny;* and to Faber and Faber Ltd. of London, for permission to use six lines from *Collected Poems* by T. S. Eliot, of which they are the publishers.

Chapter 1

TEMPTATION AND SIN

Flee from sin as from the face of a serpent; for if thou comest too near it, it will bite thee; the teeth thereof are as the teeth of a lion, slaying the souls of men.

Ecclesiasticus

THIS is a book about a very unpopular subject. Christians have always seemed to be obsessed with the subject of sin. They are often accused of placing an unhealthy emphasis upon it. Society at large tends to take a rather bland view of its conduct, and prefers to congratulate itself upon its virtues rather than to dwell overmuch upon its failings, and then along comes the Christian— a troublesome fellow—with his uncomfortable and unwelcome talk of man being a sinner in need of redemption and forgiveness. He is like the person who persistently calls attention to the fact that there is something wrong with the drains, when the other people living in the house would prefer to ignore the rather strange smells they can't help noticing from time to time, and find it much more congenial to maintain that everything is quite in order. This ill-bred insistence upon such an unpleasant matter results no doubt from a twisted personality with complexes of a dark and hidden kind.

Unfortunately, the Christian is a realist. He continues to insist that everything is very far from being in order, that try as we will to live in a world of pretense, the brute fact of sin is an inescapable one which all men must face and take into account. To ignore the existence of sin is, in fact, to do what psychologists tell us is fatal to mental health—not facing up to reality. In this book, we shall try to look clearly at this unpleasant factor in human life, to examine it, to see it for what it is, and to discover what we can do about it.

One of the first things to get clear is that temptation and sin are not the same thing at all. People are sometimes confused about this, but once we think about it, the difference is quite obvious. The author of the Epistle to the Hebrews tells us that Jesus himself was in all points tempted as we are, and yet was without sin. A temptation is a prompting in the heart, a desire in the mind to do something we know to be wrong. It is these thoughts enticing to evil that constitute temptation. We cannot always prevent their occurring to us; but, unless we give place to them, we have not fallen into sin. Sin occurs when the desire is welcomed and made at home. Suppose a young man is tempted to break into an empty store some dark evening. He knows it to be an easy job. The cash register has not been cleared and he could buy many things he would like with the proceeds. On the other hand, as an acolyte at his church, he has often heard the Ten Commandments and knows that stealing is wrong. So he walks round the block while his heart within him is sharply divided between the desire for evil and the desire for good. Perhaps he wrestles with this temptation all evening, but if, in the end, he goes home to bed without breaking into the store, he has not sinned. He has spent an evening wrestling with temptation, which is quite another matter.

Temptation comes to us in three successive stages. First, there is "awareness." In some way or another, an evil suggestion comes into the mind. The sinful idea is presented as a possible course of action. (*The store is deserted. It would be easy to break in.*) The next stage is "delight." This is usually a more or less instinctive response to the suggestion. The enemy has gained a foothold. The evil idea is not only present; it has touched a responsive chord and has become attractive. (*It would pay off well. I could make the down payment on that car.*) Now the will is involved and the soul must choose. (*I'd give anything for that car. . . . But Father Smith would be upset, and I know he's right really.*) So a third stage is reached, which is "consent," or "rejection." It is only at this point that temptation may pass into sin. Sin occurs if the will goes over to the enemy and the temptation wins the day. (*The hell with Father Smith. I'll do it.*) If the will holds fast and rejects the evil though pleasant suggestion, no sin has been committed. (*No, I won't do it. I'd better go home.*) The temptation has been resisted and one of Christ's soldiers has stood firm under fire.

The occasions of temptation, or the circumstances that lead to temptation, are of two different kinds: the primary and the secondary. The primary occasion is when the temptation is right there beside us. The secondary occasion is a situation or set of circumstances where temptation is very likely. These secondary occasions vary from one person to another. It depends where one's weakness lies. An occasion that would have no dangers for one person might be very dangerous for someone else. For a man who is inclined to drink too much, a grill or a hotel or a party would be secondary occasions of temptation. For a woman who is inclined to be extravagant, an expensive dress shop could be a secondary occasion of temptation. For a quarrelsome person, the company of people who annoy him; for a lustful person, the circumstances that would make possible the committing of that sin; for a greedy and gluttonous person, the meal table is a secondary occasion of temptation; for an envious and covetous person, the company of people better off than he. For every temptation, there is a primary and a secondary occasion, and we need to be on our guard against going blindly into secondary occasions of those temptations to which we are personally liable. Jesus said: "Watch and pray, that ye enter not into temptation." One part of being watchful is to avoid those circumstances which are secondary occasions of temptation for us. Each man must do this for himself.

Suppose there is a soldier who has to make his way toward a certain objective on the battlefield. He knows that one or two areas are particularly dangerous. He has seen a few of his comrades shot at from there, perhaps he himself has been wounded from the same direction. He is not going in that direction if he can help it. If there is another way to his objective, he'll take that instead.

We are trying to make our way toward the heavenly city. If there are some places that are especially dangerous for us, we will be best advised to avoid them if we can. Sometimes, of course, the danger will be unavoidable. We cannot cut ourselves off from the world. For politeness, or because of our friends, or because of the ordinary business of living, we shall from time to time find ourselves entering a secondary occasion of temptation, a situation or set of circumstances which are going to be especially dangerous for us. When this occurs, we need to be doubly careful and consciously on guard. "Be sober, be vigilant," wrote St. Peter; "because your adversary the Devil, as a roaring lion, walketh about, seeking whom he may devour."

Temptation then is not the same thing as sin. It is a testing, a trial of strength, and, by steadily resisting it, the soul can grow firm and strong. The reason that it so frequently leads us into acts of sin is what we must now think about.

A good definition of sin is "disobedience to the known will of

God." The word "sin" always refers to a broken relationship between man and God. We sometimes speak of "sins against society" or of a man "sinning against himself," but these are really metaphorical ways of speaking. An act committed against the laws of society is a crime; an offense against our neighbors is an injury; an offense against our own well-being is an act of folly. Only as committed against God is an act a sin. Any one of these other actions we have just mentioned may be a sin as well, and probably is, because it is God's will for us to be good citizens and good neighbors, but it is only when we are thinking about how the act will affect our relationship to God that we can say whether it is a sin or not. The word "sin" always has reference to God. It means that we have deliberately gone against his will.

Sooner or later, everybody does this. There is a fault or twist or infection (whatever you like to call it) in the human race which, given time, eventually and inevitably finds expression in acts of sin, just as the physical body eventually passes into sickness and death. This is what the Church's much misunderstood doctrine of original sin is all about. It is an attempt to express the phenomenon that all men everywhere do in fact fall into sin. Sin is universal. There is no instance of a human being without it. Universal sin must therefore receive the same interpretation that any other universal does: it implies a law in consequence of which it is universal. Nobody supposes that anything takes place universally by chance or accident. Newton noted that all objects fall, and he put forward the "law" of gravity as an expression of the underlying principle which governs this phenomenon. So the Church observes that all men sin, and puts forward the "law," which we call "original sin," to express it.

It is not only Christians who are aware of this universality of human sin. Although other words may be used to describe it, the realization of it is reflected in the literature of all races and all countries. There is a widespread sense of the dullness and heaviness of human nature, so continually falling below its best aspirations. Again and again, well-laid plans made by honest and well-meaning men split and flounder on the rock of human nature. Again and again, men's actions fail to match the ideal which would be perfectly realizable if only human nature were not what it is. St. Paul spoke for all men when he wrote, "The good that I would, I do not; but the evil that I would not, that I do." Sin is a universal experience and yet it is everywhere felt to be unnatural and below man's proper level of behavior. Men are inescapably aware that there are within them moral potentialities that demand from them a level of conduct quite different from that of other creatures. As G. K. Chesterton once wrote: "If I wish to dissuade a man from drinking his tenth whisky and soda, I slap him on the back and say, 'Be a man.' No-one who wished to dissuade a crocodile from eating its tenth explorer would slap it on the back and say, 'Be a crocodile.'"

Jesus Christ is the revelation to us of what man was made to be. When men place their lives alongside his, they realize the gulf between what they are and what they were meant to be. As Martin Luther called him with such profound truth in his great hymn "Ein feste Burg," Christ is *der rechte Mann,* the true man, or the proper man, as the usual English translation runs. Christ shows us what man was intended to be like. We need to keep clear the distinction between "normal" in the sense of what everyone does and "normal" in the sense of what man, as true man, should do and be. Some recently published studies in human social behavior have tended to obscure this distinction, and so we find people speaking as if the fact that some activity (such as, for example, casual fornication) is widespread means that it is also in keeping with man's true nature. On the contrary, human social customs tend to vary from one historical period to another, and very often a pattern of behavior that is widespread for a time is later understood to have been a violation of a fundamental law of man's being, and so to have been "abnormal" in the strictest sense of the word.

Sin is not normal for men. It is not in accordance with what man was made to do and be. It has resulted in a defacing of God's image, a spoiling of God's plan. At their best moments of courage or of self-forgetting love or of creative art, even sinful men can give us glimpses of the splendid creatures we were meant to be. When we walk through a hospital ward and see the emaciated bodies of people weakened by disease, we can still discern, even in these pitiable sick folk, the faded image of what their healthy bodies once were like. So we sinful human beings still carry about with us, though in a blurred and tarnished way, the indications of the splendid image in which we were originally made. It is our sin, our disobedience to God, that has spoiled us. Man cannot live his true life apart from union with God. Apart from God, his whole constitution has become disordered. Russian Orthodox theology has a word for this. They speak of *prelest,* which means being beguiled and taking mirages for truth. Universal sin has not only weakened our natures; it has made us incapable of seeing things as they really are, in the sight of God. Through our universal sin, we have wandered far away from our true home with him, and have exchanged life and happiness for exile and death. It is significant that the Book of Genesis opens with the thrilling words "In the beginning, God . . ." and ends with the somber ones ". . . in a coffin, in Egypt."

This doctrine of original sin is of course the very opposite of a fatalistic or pessimistic view of man. On the contrary, it provides a ground for hope which would otherwise be completely lacking. If man's normal state is to be what he now universally is, then there is no hope for him at all here or hereafter. But the Church's teaching is precisely that his true nature is to be something quite different. It holds out the possibility of his being rescued and restored and this is what it was that Christ came to do. How we may take advantage of Christ's redemptive and rescuing work on our behalf is the subject of the last chapter in this book, entitled "The Way Back," but first, we must take a clear, cold look at this web of universal sin in which all of us are caught up together. Once we understand our true situation, we begin to appreciate God's goodness in sending his Son to rescue us from it. The man who knows himself to be a sinner is grateful for God's mercy; the smug and complacent see nothing to be grateful for. The Church has to preach the Bad News about men so that they will listen to the Good News about God.

Although we are all born into this condition of universal sinfulness, we are not, of course, personally responsible for it. Christians believe in original sin, not in original guilt. Guilt comes in only when the sin becomes actual, when, of our own free will, we personally yield to temptation and choose the wrong.

Individual acts of sin are to original sin as the fruit is to a tree. They are the evil results of the root sinfulness that we have just been considering. If the works of a clock are out of order, the hands will show the wrong time. We may correct them, and they may stay nearly right for a time, but, sooner or later, they will go wrong again because the basic trouble is still there. Actual sins are the fruit which grows from the tree of original sin. They are the actual manifestations in everyday life of the basic and univeral sinfulness of the human race.

They are not all of equal seriousness. You remember that we defined sin as "disobedience to the known will of God." Some acts of disobedience are more deliberate than others. All parents know this. Here is one boy. In a moment of thoughtless excitement in trying out a new baseball bat in the yard, Bob hits a superb and soul-satisfying ball which unfortunately ends up outside the yard and through a neighbor's window. Bob's father is going to be justifiably annoyed. No doubt the boy will have to pay for the damage from his pocket money. But there has been no real intention to disobey. The fault has resulted from the thoughtless excitement of the moment, and although punishment may follow, no harm has been done to the loving relationship between father and son. Here is another boy. There have recently been some unpleasant occasions of boys and girls found drinking and petting in cars on the outskirts of town. Bill's father has once or twice warned him that this gang was no good and has advised him to avoid them. Bill has always readily agreed and has repeatedly said that he certainly would never go along with that kind of behavior. Then, Bill's father misses different sums of money from his desk, and in checking up, gradually comes to understand, by investigations here and there, that all the time that Bill has been giving him the assurances he has wanted to hear, the boy has in fact been one of the worst of the gang and has even boasted openly of the sucker he had for a father. This second case is quite different from the first. Here, there has been cold, calculating, and unloving disobedience. Against his father's known wishes, the son has set his own intention to deceive and to disobey. The resultant damage to the relationship between them is serious and deep.

It is the same with us and God. Some sins are done thoughtlessly, with no deliberate intention to offend. We slip into them almost before we realize what we are doing. They are imperfections by which we fall short of the absolute standard of obedience which we know we owe to God. The Church has a name for these thoughtless sins. They are called venial sins. They are not the result of deliberate disobedience and so do not involve a very serious break in our relationship with God. But some sins are what the Church calls mortal sins. They are "sins done with a high hand." The soul has deliberately gone over to the enemy. The disobedience is with full knowledge and consent, and the breach with the Heavenly Father is consequently deep and serious. This division of sins into venial and mortal is a common-sense one; but it is often difficult to say into which class a particular act of sin will fall. This varies from person to person. But it is useful to remember that not all sins are of equal seriousness; what matters is how deliberate our disobedience has been.

Chapter 2

THE SEVEN ROOT SINS

Now they be called chieftains, for as much as they be chief, and from them spring all other sinnes. The root of these sinnes then is Pride, the general root of all harmes. From this root spring certain branches: as ire, envy, sloth, avarice, gluttony, lechery; and each of these chief sinnes hath his branches and his twigges.

Chaucer, *Canterbury Tales*

THE individual sinful acts that men commit seem to spring from certain root, or capital sins. With a little study, practice, and observation, it is possible to recognize these different types of sin as we meet them in ourselves and others. This is a sin of pride; that is a sin of gluttony; this other results from envy; this fourth is a manifestation of the root sin of anger; this fifth springs from lust. Each particular root sin produces a certain kind of character, and each gives rise to individual acts of sin which are recognizably of the same type. Most of us have more than one or two of these evil weeds rooted within us. To recognize their fruit when we see it is a step forward in self-knowledge, and in the direction of that personal holiness which is at once the goal and the requirement that the Master sets before each of us.

As early as the beginning of the second century A.D., there was a start made in the direction of recognizing these main roots of sin. An early Christian document, of unknown authorship, called the *Didache,* contains a list of five. As the next century opened, Origen took the work a further step forward and produced a sevenfold list in which five of our present seven are included. Toward the end of the fourth century, a monk named Cassian put forward an amended sevenfold list. Cassian's list was almost exactly followed by Gregory the Great, two hundred years later, when he wrote his *Moralia in Job* (a devotional commentary on the Book of Job). In the thirty-first chapter of this work, Gregory gave us what has become the classic exposition of the subject.

Gregory's list, which has long been accepted as the traditional one, runs as follows: pride, envy, anger, sloth, avarice, gluttony, lust. When commenting on verse 25 of chapter 39 in the Book of Job ("the thunder of the captains and the shouting"), he likens the seven capital sins to captains laying waste a conquered city, each leading after him his band of following vices. "An army in truth follows those captains because there spring up from them importunate hosts of sins—These several sins have each their army against us—Seven principal vices produce from themselves so great a multitude of vices that when they reach the heart they bring, as it were, the bands of an army after them."

Gregory lived long before modern psychological discoveries about the way in which human nature works. He would certainly not have understood words like "rationalization"; but all the same he was well aware of the way in which men like to dress up their sins as virtues and to present them in a reasonable, or at least an excusable, light. After uncompromisingly identifying the sins in his book, he goes on to show how each one comes provided with an argument by which it tries to make itself seem entirely right and proper.

He makes each of the seven sins speak insinuatingly in turn. Although the arguments were written fourteen hundred years ago, there is a remarkably modern ring about them. They include the same ways in which we try to justify these same sins to ourselves today.

PRIDE: You ought to aim at greater things, so that, when you have been able to surpass many other people in power, then you will be able to use your power to benefit many people also.

ENVY: In what way are you inferior to this or that person? Why then are you not treated as either equal or superior to them? Think of the great things that you are able to do and which they are not able to do! They ought not then to be regarded as either superior, or even equal, to you.

ANGER: The things that are done to you cannot be borne patiently. Indeed, to bear them patiently would be wrong; because if you do not indignantly withstand them, they will later be heaped upon you without measure.

MELANCHOLY SLOTH: What reason have you to be happy, when you endure so many wrongs from your neighbors? What cause you have for sorrow when you reflect how bitterly everyone acts towards you!

AVARICE: It is certainly a very blameless thing that you desire to own a few possessions. It is not that you want to be rich but that you merely wish to avoid being in want. Those possessions which that person there keeps for no good purpose, you yourself could use much better than he does.

GLUTTONY: God has created all good food and drink. He who refuses to fill himself with food, what else is he doing but refusing the gifts of God?

LUST: Why not enjoy yourself now, because you do not know

what the future may bring! You ought not to waste the time you have, because you do not know how quickly it may pass away. If it were not right for men to enjoy sexual intercourse, God would not at the first beginning of the human race have made them male and female.

These are the words which Gregory used fourteen hundred years ago. The disguises are much the same as those in which the sins present themselves to us nowadays. Each age has found little difficulty in inventing polite euphemisms suited to its own time. The sins have varied in order of popularity from one century to another, and from one nation to another; but in one form or another they have remained firmly embedded in human nature. The modern phrases by which a person excuses them to himself perhaps run like this:

PRIDE: I ought to take my proper place (in society, in my club, in my firm). I have many natural gifts (good looks, business ability, physical strength—whatever it is that he fancies in himself) which ought to receive recognition. Once I've got ahead, I'll be able to do a great deal of good too, and give much wiser leadership than those people who are calling themselves leaders right now. [Of course, he won't really do as much good as he makes himself think, probably no more than anyone else who might have held the same position. Power corrupts, and once a man has thrust himself forward to a position of power, a good deal of his interest becomes devoted to preserving and enjoying it.]

ENVY: I just want what is only fair. I'm just as hardworking (or clever, or well-educated, or strong, or good-looking, or deserving in any way you like to mention) as that other fellow. In fact, in many ways I'm a great deal better. [The ways, if any, in which he excels are likely to be less important and less numerous than he thinks.] People admire that fellow altogether too much when they really ought to admire me. This feeling of dislike that I have for him only results from my perfectly natural desire for fair play.

ANGER: Am I a man or a mouse? If I let him get away with treating me like that, he'll be worse next time. If I don't stand up for myself and tell that fellow where he gets off, no one else is going to do it for me. I'll give him a piece of my mind. Who does he think he is, treating me like that? It'll be a useful lesson for him. In fact, not to have a row with him would be weakness on my part, and would only encourage him to continue to act like that. The more I think of it, the more I see that I *ought* to have a good row with him. (It'll make me feel much better, too.)

SLOTH: I'm tired. I'm fed up. Everything seems to have gone against me for a long time now. It's all very well, when you're young and idealistic, to dream about reforms and splendid achievements and all that. But a few years' experience of the real world shows an intelligent man that everything's really a racket. Enthusiasm is for fanatics. I'll dismiss anything of that kind with a cynical wisecrack. It'll get a laugh and it'll get me out of it anyway.

AVARICE: If I could just put my hands on a little more money per annum, I'd be O.K. I don't want to be really rich [like anyone you care to mention who is earning about ten thousand more than he is at the moment]. It's just that there are a few things I really would enjoy [a fishing rod, a cabin cruiser, a castle in Spain—it depends at what level he is]. Once I got these, I wouldn't want anything more. [Oh, wouldn't he!]

GLUTTONY: I'm a man who enjoys good living. And why not? I work hard. [He thinks he does anyway.] Why shouldn't I indulge myself a bit? I remember even reading in the Bible that the enemies of Jesus called him a gluttonous man and a wine-bibber. He wasn't, of course. He just enjoyed the good things of life, the way I do. Perfectly justifiable. I like a man who can take a few drinks and can appreciate a good dinner.

LUST: Puritanical kill-joys take all the pleasure out of life. It's unhealthy and unnatural for a man to live like a monk. It only backs up on him and comes out in other ways. If two people enjoy having a bit of fun together, why shouldn't they? They're not doing anyone else any harm. Thank heaven we've escaped from old-fashioned taboos about this. It's just a healthy expression of a basic human instinct. If you want some learned arguments about it, I can easily show you plenty of important writers who will tell you the same thing. So come on, why not?

The familiar phrase "the seven deadly sins" is a little misleading. In the previous chapter, we saw the distinction between deadly (or mortal) and venial sins. Doesn't the Church regard cruelty or lying as a deadly sin, people may ask. The answer is that of course both of these sins are deadly to the soul which gives way to them and upon which they fasten their fatal evil grip; but neither of them is a root sin. For example, no one tells lies for the sake of telling lies, but because some deeper sinfulness prompts the lies in the first place. The act of lying may, in fact, be the result of any one of the seven root sins. A man may tell lies in order to make himself seem more important (pride), or to take away someone else's good reputation (envy), or to injure someone he hates (wrath), or to escape a duty (sloth), or to put through a dishonest deal in business (covetousness), or to excuse a self-indulgence (gluttony), or to seduce a woman (lust). To deal only with the sin of lying would be to deal with the symptom instead of with the basic sickness. The seven deadly sins may be described as the seven roots of wickedness in human nature, which find expression in individual acts of sin.

Each sin has its characteristic "children," which belong to the same family and spring from a common parent. Human beings vary between themselves, and so, with different people, the same visible act of sin may come from different roots. But, on the whole, it is possible to make a list of sins which derive from each root sin and which are the characteristic expressions of it:

Pride: presumption, hypocrisy, obstinacy, quarrelsomeness, disobedience, boasting, ostentation, lack of consideration for others.

Envy: hatred, falsehood, calumny, evil interpretation, contempt, whisperings, slanders, detractions, pleasure at a neighbor's misfortune and sorrow at his prosperity.

Anger: resentment, ingratitude, suspicion, rancor, mental agitation, insults, indignation, blasphemy.

Sloth: hatred of spiritual things, moral cowardice, cynicism, despair, weakness in prayer, laziness, a wandering of the mind on unlawful matters.

Covetousness: anxiety, fraud, deceit, perjury, dishonesty, callousness, fear of loss, treachery, a hardness of heart against compassion.

Gluttony: drunkenness, foolish mirth, scurrility, uncleanness, impurity, love of ease, dullness in understanding, lack of appreciation of higher things, betraying of secrets.

Lust: contempt for spiritual things, fornication, marital infidelity, seduction, cruelty, blindness of mind, a coarsening of the nature, a dehumanizing way of treating members of the opposite sex.

The selection of seven sins as the root ones was probably somewhat influenced by the fact that "seven" was regarded as a mystical number. But the traditional list is a valid one. These evil roots are in fact mankind's fundamental sinful dispositions which manifest themselves in various ways. Conversely, the visible acts of sin are indications of what is within, just as, says Chaucer's Parson in his Tale, the sign outside the tavern is the sign of the wine that is in the cellar.

Reference is made to the seven root sins in many famous books of the Western world. Dante's treatment of the subject in his "Purgatory," the second book of the *Divine Comedy,* is perhaps the best known and the most profound. Led by Virgil, the poet passes slowly up the mountain, being purged from each of the seven sins in turn. Virgil points out to him (Cantos 17 and 18) that as love is the basic driving-force of all virtue, so love-gone-wrong is the driving-force of all sin. Each of the seven sins is shown to be love in some disordered, perverted, or excessive form. Men sometimes twist a right and natural love away from its natural object and direct it to an unnatural and perverted object. For example, the envious man perverts the love of his own good (a natural and healthy love) into a desire to deprive other men of theirs. At other times, men fail to keep a proper priority among the objects of their desire. The pleasures of good food and drink, for example, are natural and healthy. But the gluttonous man has allowed his love of this natural pleasure to become excessive, and so unnatural. Love gone wrong in some way is at the root of all the seven sins. It is worth noticing that the first five are all spiritual sins, and only the last two are sins of the flesh. Dante clearly regarded the last two as deadly, but less hard to eradicate than the other five.

To Dante belongs also the credit for recognizing that the spiritual axioms which we call the Beatitudes are almost exact counterparts to these root sins. It is not surprising that this is so; in those famous sayings that form part of his Sermon on the Mount, our Lord was enunciating the requirements for a blessed and happy human life. He introduced each one with the word "blessed" (*makarios*). This Greek word could equally well be translated "happy," and is in fact so translated elsewhere in the King James Version of the Bible. Our Lord is saying not only that the man who acts according to these principles is "blessed" or approved by God, but also that he will be a truly happy man. The Beatitudes go against much that the world counts as wisdom but in fact they are signposts to a happy life for those who are wise enough to follow them. Whatever the world may say, there is no division between goodness and happiness. On the contrary, they go together like two sides of the same penny. The good man is a happy man. Although sin may appear to do so on the surface, it does not in fact provide a path to happiness. Sin is a deceiver; it is death pretending to be life. The word "makarios" emphasizes the truth that happiness is to be found finally nowhere but in the will of God. As we come to consider each of the root sins, we shall look briefly also at the contrary Beatitude and see how our Lord's teaching strikes at each root of human wickedness (and human unhappiness) in turn:

Against pride: Blessed are the meek
Against envy: Blessed are the merciful
Against anger: Blessed are the peacemakers
Against sloth: Blessed are they that mourn
Against covetousness: Blessed are the poor in spirit
Against gluttony: Blessed are they that hunger and thirst after righteousness
Against lust: Blessed are the pure in heart

When looked at from another angle, each of these root sins

can be seen as a natural human instinct that has gone astray. As Duns Scotus said: No vice is found but is the shadow of some virtue. (*De Divina Natura,* I. 68.)

There is a basic need for self-expression and self-assertion. A person needs to feel significant, to know that he is doing something worthwhile with his life. This important and valuable drive in the human personality has produced the great advances in the history of mankind, as well as being the mainspring of most people's working lives. It must be satisfied if a man is to be a real man, or a woman a real woman. But if it turns inward and becomes directed toward an introverted self-gratification, it degenerates into pride.

Pugnacity is the quality that makes a person able to stand bravely against opposition, to hold firm in the face of difficulty, to persevere in what he feels to be right, to carry something through to successful completion. Little can be accomplished by someone in whom this important quality is lacking. But if it turns inward and becomes self-regarding, it finds expression as the root sin of anger and becomes the cause of many surface sins of personal wrath and bad temper.

There is an instinct for acquisitiveness in human nature. The small boy collects birds' eggs or bottle tops. The little girl may collect prettily colored pebbles or beads. The collections of older people are bewildering in their variety and are often pursued with a wealth of learned interest that amuses the outsider. Postage stamps, coins, matchcovers, clocks, pictures, old furniture, first editions, the list is endless. To admire something that seems desirable to us and then to wish to possess it is a drive that appears to be common to most of us. In moderation, there is nothing harmful here. It has given much pleasure to many people, and over the years has resulted in the collecting together of many beautiful objects which others can conveniently see and enjoy. Those of us who are not collectors in the narrow sense usually enjoy acquiring things for our homes or for our families. This can lead to the virtues of thrift and sensible self-discipline as we go without this or that in order to acquire the desired. When this instinct of acquisitiveness becomes perverted, however, it turns into that never satisfied desire to possess for the sake of exclusive possession which is the essence of covetousness.

The root sin of envy is a combination of perverted acquisitiveness and perverted self-assertion. A desire for exclusive possession is enforced by an introverted drive to succeed. So the unfortunate person who happens to have what we want becomes the object of our envy and dislike. We are thwarted, and we make ourselves feel better by attacking the man or woman who seems to us to be the cause of this uncomfortable feeling.

Down the ages, when men have looked out upon the limitless expanse of a desert, or upward toward the peaks of a majestic mountain range, or at a tossing succession of waves reaching to the horizon on all sides, they have experienced a feeling of self-abasement and humility. These negative self-feelings, as they are sometimes called, are another ingredient in human personality. It is right that this should be. Man is in fact quite a weak, small, and relatively insignificant phenomenon in nature. He is wise to recognize the fact. His mightiest works can be swept away in a moment's earthquake. The jungle quickly returns over his cities once the civilization that supported them has had its day. Man must therefore come to terms with the world and appreciate his own limitations. But he must not give in and despair. There is much that he can do, and he must do what he can. Otherwise, negative self-feelings degenerate into sloth or *accidie,* that dull state of soul where nothing has any meaning and no action is worth taking.

We must eat and drink in order to live. The instinct for food is basic and the need for food is the motivating force of much of the world's labor. But when food ceases to be a means to the end of living and becomes an end in itself, divorced from its real purpose, the instinct is perverted into gluttony.

Sexual union must take place in order for the human race to continue. By this means, two human beings can be used to bring a third into existence. They procreate. They act on behalf of God. No doubt for biological reasons, the act of procreation is an intensely enjoyable one. But if the desire for it is turned inward and becomes concerned only with selfish enjoyment, the sex instinct has degenerated into lust.

One word of warning to you who are reading this book. As we now pass each of these root sins in review, we should be looking all the time to see how far they have taken root in our own hearts. Don't let us spend too much time recognizing them in other people. This would be both easy and enjoyable, but it is not what this book is written for. When a man reads a medical book, he fancies that he has every disease he finds described there; but let him read a work like this, and all the sins pointed out he sees not in himself, but in his neighbors. Never mind about your neighbors. How far can you find yourself here?

Chapter 3

PRIDE

And though so be that no man knoweth utterly the number of the twigges and of the harmes that come of Pride, yet will I show a part of them, as ye shall understand. There is inobedience, vaunting, hypocrisy, despite, arrogance, impudence, swelling of heart, insolence, elation, impatience, strife, contumacy, presumption, irreverence, stubbornness, vain glorie, and many other twigges that I cannot declare.

Chaucer, *Canterbury Tales*

The Contrary Virtue to Pride is Humility

Blessed are the meek

In a sense, pride is the root sin at the root of all the others because it consists essentially in putting the great inflated ME in the center of our life—a place that should be reserved for God only. It is the sin of pretending to be as God and of supposing that we can do without him. It is interesting to notice that in the classic account of human temptation given us in the Genesis story of Adam and Eve, it was exactly along these lines that Satan made his subtle and successful approach to Eve. "Ye shall be as God," he whispered insinuatingly.

The desire to be clever enough to be able to dispense with God is the beginning of the slippery path that leads downward into the special hell of pride where it is always "I" who is right; "I" who never has a chance; "I" who is misunderstood. It isn't fair; people have never properly appreciated me; I have a right to have a grudge against the universe which has never treated me as well as I really deserve; it isn't fair. So, like the gluttonous, envious, or lustful man, the man consumed by pride has a wretched pretaste on earth of the hell that he is preparing for himself. A bitter hell of consuming self-pity results from the fact that other people unaccountably decline to join him in that worship of himself which is the central element of his sin.

The root sin of pride shows itself in many ways, some very destructive and unpleasant, some comparatively harmless and even amusing to other people. It is sometimes said that pride has three children: presumption, an overweening desire to excel, and vanity.

Presumption is a desire for things that are too lofty for us. The presumptuous man has such a good opinion of himself that he is not aware of any deficiency whatever in his own abilities. He has no hesitation in vigorously advancing his opinions on any topic that may arise, however little he may really know about it. He advises his doctor authoritatively on medical treatments, his child's teacher on educational methods, his city council on town planning, and his rector on how to run the parish. He writes frequently to the newspapers. He can be distinguished from the serious, public-minded and worthy citizen (who occasionally may quite rightly do all of these things), by the eagerness with which he hastens to display his airy and self-assured om-

34

niscience. His name is Mr. Know-all, and a tiresome neighbor for anyone. Another form of presumption causes a man to desire positions in life for which he is not fitted. His worship of himself is so intense that he cannot see that other men have qualifications that he does not have. And so he pushes his way toward positions in his company, or offices in his community, which other people can clearly see he is incapable of holding successfully. When he is rejected, or worse still when he is appointed and then inevitably fails, he sees the reasons for his failure everywhere but in himself. He is the victim of bad luck, of lack of co-operation, of jealousy. So he starts on the slippery slope into self-pity. It is unthinkable that the image of himself should be a false one. The reason that other people do not worship it along with him is their blindness or spite.

Mr. Wilbur Jones had had a good year. The contracting business that he had inherited from his father had benefited from the local housing boom and he was showing a nice profit on the season's work. Mrs. Jones, who had majored in French at college, talked him into a trip to Europe, which was something that several of her neighbors had already taken and something after which she had consequently yearned for some time. So off they went. So far as Wilbur was concerned, the best thing about it was the boat trip each way. He had been raised in the Middle West and the sights, sounds, and smells of shipboard life were a holiday to him in themselves. His wife was made of sterner stuff. From the moment they landed, their six-weeks' stay, from Wilbur's point of view, became a kaleidoscopic whirl of art galleries, gourmet restaurants, cultural concerts, old castles, and cathedrals. He was glad to get back home. So was Mrs. Jones, but for a different reason. The fact that her memories of college French had proved to be of unaccountably little value among the slow-witted inhabitants of that country was not enlarged upon. Her pride, which was the basic urge that had taken them to Europe in the first place, did not permit even a humorous account of her linguistic inadequacies. The picture that she built up among the members of her Thursday bridge club was a more flattering one. Travel enlarges the mind. It enlarged Mrs. Jones's. She became an authority on out-of-the-way European resorts, not as yet spoiled by American tourists; she fell into the habit of forming the figure 7 in the French manner; much to Wilbur's chagrin, she took to patronizing the delicatessen store recently opened a few blocks away by an enterprising immigrant couple from Hungary; copies of illustrated French, German, and Italian magazines were usually to be seen on the coffee table in the living room.

Her pride drew her more and more deeply into presumption as, in order to project her chosen image of herself, she laid claim to knowledge, tastes, and experience which in reality she did not possess. She achieved some occasional moments of pleasure when the more polite or more simple-minded of her friends received her performance with friendly indulgence; but for the most part she aroused impatience and resentment. No one likes being used as part of the scenery to set off the brilliant figure in the center of the stage. It seemed to Mrs. Jones that her friends were becoming more envious and spiteful than they had used to be. That fall, she was not re-elected as Vice-President of the Ladies' Aid. The number of her friends was in fact diminishing sharply and she herself might have become quite hardened in presumption and pride when, as it happened, Wilbur's partner's wife died suddenly, leaving three small children. A kindly and sympathetic woman at heart, Mrs. Jones came to the rescue. Her days became full of child diets, diapers, cut fingers, money-for-milk-at-school, and a hundred and one such matters. Although she made a conscientious attempt for some time to retain the lovely picture of herself as a woman with cosmopolitan interests, the imaginary inevitably gave way before the real. The presumptuous image of herself gradually and imperceptibly faded. She was delivered into self-forgetfulness, which is the heart of humility and the contrary virtue that drives out pride.

The second child of pride is overweening desire to excel. This shows itself in an inordinate love of attention and the limelight, of honors and dignities, of positions of authority and control over others. A desire to do well is wholesome and good; but the mainspring of the life of the man suffering from this form of pride is the desire to feed his own self-importance by doing

better than other people. He must be at the head table, he must
meet the guest of honor, his wife must be one of the best-dressed,
his car one of the glossiest. If he plays bridge, he must win;
if he bowls, he can't rest until he is made the team's captain.
The professional at a golf club I know once told me of a successful business executive who decided to take up the game and
came to him for lessons. The professional gave him a full course
of instruction and the man set out to play. He shot well over a
hundred for a few rounds and came back for more lessons.
Obligingly my friend gave him a little brush-up on what he had
already taught him and sent him off again. By relentless practice
and grim, joyless determination, our hero brought his average
score down to the low nineties; and there he stuck. He was a
middle-aged man, not particularly athletic, and that was just
about as well as he could reasonably hope to do. But all around
him, he saw young men shooting in the eighties and even men of
his own age (who had been playing for years) doing equally
well. After a few months, he gave up the game and resigned
from the club. He could find no pleasure in it unless he could
excel. The fresh air, the friendly companionship, the satisfaction
of playing well by his own standard, could not outweigh the un-
endurable fact that others were doing better than he. The man
who is the victim of an overweening desire to excel is never
able to be hidden or to be in a subordinate position. Our Western civilization tends to breed him. His name is Mr. Got-to-win.
His coat of arms is an ulcer rampant on a sea of high blood
pressure.

The third child of pride is vanity—an inordinate desire to be
thought well of. As with all the other sins, this is a twisting or
warping of something that is perfectly good and healthy in itself.
The vain man is not content with his fair share of affection and
appreciation; he must always be calling attention to his supposed
virtues. He must somehow turn every story to show himself in
a favorable light, just a little shrewder, braver, wittier, or better-
connected than he really is. He is a great name-dropper. We
are never left unaware of any important people he has met or
impressive places he has visited. Sometimes his minor personal

vanities make us smile privately to ourselves, but he himself cannot endure to be laughed at. The image of himself is too sacred to be the object of ridicule.

> I love to watch the rooster crow.
> He's like so many men I know,
> Who brag and bluster, rant and shout,
> And beat their manly chests without
> The first darn thing to brag about.

A year or two ago, I happened to be changing planes at a small and not very important northern Canadian town. The quite inadequate terminal building was crowded with the thirty or so passengers who were waiting. We were a nondescript and humdrum collection of human beings for the most part: lumbermen, miners, perhaps a schoolteacher or a nurse or two, possibly a couple of junior salesmen, and myself, a middle-sized, middle-aged clergyman. It was the late fall and the early snow was already on the ground. Most of us were wearing snowshoes, parkas and fur caps with ear flaps. A typical rather drab workaday group of average people. But in the center of the little room stood an exotic figure: a small dark man with a carefully trained Van Dyke beard, an overcoat with a velvet collar, and a scarf flung back over his shoulder. He was maintaining a conversation in a high-pitched voice with a striking looking woman, while manipulating a cigarette in a long holder. He was an *outré* figure in such a place. As I watched him from a corner of the room, his occasional quick side glances from side to side showed that he was aware of and pleased by the effect he was creating. He almost visibly savored the delicious sense of being the center of attraction. After a quarter of an hour, our second plane arrived and the little incident was over. He would have passed from my memory were it not for the coincidence that a few days later, I happened to watch a television quiz show and saw him again as one of the members of the panel. I have forgotten his name and would not, of course, reveal it here even if I remembered it. He was a minor literary celebrity. As I listened to the opinions he delivered with a sublime confidence on a variety of subjects to a respectful moderator, I could not forget that chance occasion at the airport a few days before when he had unconsciously revealed himself to at least one observer as a vain and posturing little man. Our private vanities are not always as private as we would wish them to be.

Vanity often shows itself in an excessive care for clothes and personal appearance. May a mere male writer suggest that this is a form of pride which is rather often found among women?

Jennifer was growing up. It did not seem so very long ago that she had been a gawky colt-legged girl with bangs and braces on her teeth. Now she seemed to have suddenly acquired a new grace of form and movement. Thin angularity had given way to slender roundness; an awkward young girl had changed almost overnight into a cool and poised young woman. Jennifer herself was far from unaware that something had happened. Her mirror spoke to her of it; the newly appraising glances of men she met spoke to her of it; the occasional, exciting, but carefully ignored wolf-whistle in the street shouted to her about it. The world was suddenly a very pleasant and stimulating place. Jennifer had become a strikingly lovely young woman. It was inevitable that she should be aware of this, but unfortunately she preened herself upon it, took a kind of personal credit for it, spent most of her waking hours savoring it, dressing it, painting it, curling it, powdering it, pinning it up, taking it down, worshipping it in the mirror, and displaying it in those ways and places where the incense of flattery and compliment was most likely to be had.

She was lovely to look at certainly. This was good. Her beauty was the gift of God to be appreciated and be thankful for. But Jennifer was in danger of spoiling it by her gross awareness of it all the time and by her view of it which inclined her to think that she was in some way entitled to take the credit personally. The spiritual path of a pretty girl is not an easy one. She often gets her own way too easily because she looks so charming. Her beauty gives her a powerful advantage over her less gifted sisters, and she can often use this advantage for selfish ends. There will always be flattering people who will encourage her to do so. Jennifer was among dangers of these kinds. Her school work suffered; she became arrogant and ill-tempered with the other members of her family (they were less inclined to adulation than the world outside) ; although she was a competent violinist she lost interest in her music; her prayers and her church grew stale and meaningless; nothing seemed so important as that people should see and admire her and her beautiful clothes. She was in fact consumed by vanity.

Her rector had known and liked her for years. She had come up through all the grades of Sunday School, and he had prepared her for Confirmation only a few years before. He understood something of what was taking place inside Jennifer. He understood also that it was right that she should wish to clothe as becomingly as possible the lovely body that God had given her. Yet how to teach her to do this and still be free from vanity? There came the night of the high-school graduation. Jennifer's dress was to be one of her loveliest. Even the rector heard about it from Jennifer's mother whom he chanced to meet in the street. That evening, while she was getting ready, a note was delivered at her house. On it was written one sentence: "O God, I thank you for making me and my graduation dress, and I offer myself to you in it." Below this, the rector had written: "To be said when you have dressed." Jennifer used the prayer as he suggested and on that graduation night she took her first steps in learning where the praise for her beauty really belonged.

A form of vanity that is particularly found among church people is perhaps worth mentioning for that reason. Sometimes it happens that someone has planned to carry out a certain piece of work for the church and then finds that someone else has already done it. If he is angered when he finds this out, it shows that mingled with his concern that the work should be done was also the less reputable motive that his own vanity should be gratified in the doing of it. For us of the clergy, pride takes the form of letting ourselves loom large in our ministry, instead of Christ our Master. If people compliment us, it is not always easy to give God the glory. From this sin of pride comes the tendency we have to take setbacks in our work as personal affronts to ourselves. We are not unlike the donkey in G. K. Chesterton's poem. He thought that the shouts and the palms were for him when they were really for the Christ whom he carried. We need to be always reminding ourselves that it is his work that we do, not our own.

We have taken a glance at some of the ordinary everyday manifestations of pride because these are the forms in which we commonly encounter it. But it is a universal and deeply rooted sin, a consuming passion reaching down into the very depths of human nature itself. The myths, legends, and stories that come down to us, from before the dawn of history and since, bear witness to the reality of this dark element in man's personality. The Greeks personified it as the nymph Hubris who, when she touched men, drove them to insane excesses of pride and insolence. Then in turn, another nymph, Nemesis, brought down inevitable judgment and punishment from heaven. Legend and story mix as ancient writings record the destructive history of pride as it takes expression in the lives of men. Prometheus defied the gods and stole the fire which Zeus had denied to mankind. His punishment was an eagle who perpetually gnawed at his vitals. Satan fell from heaven through pride. The sin of Adam was the desire to "be as God." The truth underlying the story of the tower of Babel is that when men's pride causes them to overreach themselves, they fall inevitably into confusion and ruin. In our own day, we hear the claim advanced or the desire expressed that man shall presently come to know everything there is to know about the nature of things. The view that man is even capable of this is a modern example of this ancient sin. It may bring its Nemesis in ways which are not looked for.

This root sin of pride issues out into a thousand different manifestations but all are alike in that the proud person is at all times trying to pretend that man, who is just a vessel formed by the Master Potter, has some kind of reason to regard himself as responsible for such virtues and talents as he happens to possess, and even has the ability to reach out toward equality with the Potter himself. He is setting up the idol of himself and forgetting that God alone is the source of all power and excellence. In his *Moralia in Job* (XXIV, 48), St. Gregory has a memorable description of the proud man. "He walks with himself along the broad spaces of his thought and silently utters his own praises." This picture catches something of the essentially haughty and narcissistic loneliness of pride. He is as a man pacing the battlements of a city, or walking in solitary silence across a wide and wintry plain. He deliciously savors the incense of his own self-worship.

Pride feeds upon a person's comparison of himself with others and so, wherever people meet with each other, there is an occasion and opportunity for this sin to wrap its evil toils around its habitual victims. "Pride," wrote Richard Hooker, "is a vice which cleaveth so fast unto the hearts of men, that if we were to strip ourselves of all faults one by one, we should undoubtedly find it the very last and hardest to put off."

The contrary virtue to pride is humility. St. Anthony was the first of the "desert fathers," as they are called. These anchorites went apart into the desert to work out their salvation "alone to the alone." From their writings come many stories of the devil's temptations, some (it perhaps seems to us today) explicable chiefly in terms of Freudian psychology, but many containing enduring spiritual insights of great worth. It is said that, on one occasion, St. Anthony saw the whole earth covered with snares, so that it appeared to him as if no one could walk in the world without falling into them. He cried, "Who can escape them all, O Lord?" The answer came, "Humility."

We cannot expect humility to be a popular virtue because pride is such a popular sin; but it has been made unnecessarily unattractive by the mistaken ideas that many people have about it. There is the canting hypocritical humility of the type of Uriah Heep. The ordinary man quite rightly finds this disgusting. It is a thousand miles removed from true humility. As pride consists of putting the great inflated ME in the center of things, so the humble man is concerned not with himself at all, but with God and other people. The humble person is the self-forgetful person. Some people seem to imagine that if they want to be humble they have to go about pretending to themselves that they really are not so good-looking, or so musically gifted, or such a good housekeeper as they know very well they actually are. Being humble is not indulging in some kind of dishonest spiritual double talk. It is simply giving the honor and credit to God from whom all excellence flows. The Virgin Mary gives us an example of true humility in her lovely song which the Church knows as the Magnificat. She has been chosen from all womankind to be the mother of God's Son. She does not shut her eyes to the fact that all mankind will forever afterward honor her and call her blessed. "My soul doth magnify the Lord . . . for he hath regarded the low estate of his handmaiden: for, behold, from henceforth all generations shall call me blessed. For he that is mighty hath done to me great things: and holy is his Name." She is free both from pride and from false humility. She does not pretend that her honor is due to herself, nor does she pretend that it does not exist. She takes an adoring delight in it because it is God's doing.

Humility is in fact a most attractive virtue but most people do not recognize it when they come across it, because they suppose humility to be something else. The humble man is interested in you and not in himself. He is an altogether delightful companion. He is pleased to listen to your news; he is as glad at your good fortune as if it had happened to himself; he advances his opinions courteously and can support them with reasons he has obviously thought about; he is happy to serve in a minor capacity on your committee but will be quite ready to accept a position of responsibility if you ask him to; he plays to win but loses gracefully if necessary. He is a patient man, quite willing to wait his turn when road construction ties up the traffic or there is a long line at a ferry. He is a self-forgetful person because he does not think of himself as being of any particular importance and because his main interests lie elsewhere. Humility, being self-forgetfulness, is not something that we can achieve directly. It is something into which we are delivered, as a by-product of something else. This is really only another way of saying that a man cannot save himself; he can only be saved.

The humble man is not a servile, grovelling person but a man who looks beyond himself for the strength he needs to live. There is the humility of the slave which looks downward. Christian humility is that of the child which looks upward, away from the self to a heavenly Father. This truth lies behind our Lord's warning: "Except ye be converted, and become as little children, ye shall not enter into the Kingdom of Heaven." This is not a call to childishness and infantilism. It is a call to be childlike, to be humble before God, as a good child is humble before his parents.

Our Lord is the perfect example of the strong, virile and yet humble man. His life and death are a standing rebuke to every form of pride to which men are liable:

Pride of birth and rank: Is not this the carpenter's son?

Pride of wealth: The Son of Man hath not where to lay his head.

Pride of respectability: Can there any good thing come out of Nazareth?

Pride of personal appearance: He hath no form nor comeliness.

Pride of reputation: A friend of publicans and sinners!

Pride of learning: How knoweth this man letters, never having learned?

Pride of superiority: I am among you as he that serveth.

Pride of success: He came unto his own and his own received him not. . . . Neither did his brethren believe in him. . . . He is despised and rejected of men.

Pride of ability: I can of mine own self do nothing.

Pride of self-will: I seek not mine own will, but the will of him that sent me.

Pride of intellect: As my Father hath taught me, I speak these things.

Pride in death: He was crucified between two thieves.

When the disciples gathered in that upper room for the Last Supper, they were too poor to afford a servant to wash their feet and too proud to do it for each other. So the Lord of Heaven and Earth did it for them. To those of us who would follow him, taking up the towel is necessary, as well as taking up the cross.

If we would learn humility, we must learn to love hiddenness, to live a life which is hidden with Christ in God, to nourish an enclosed garden of the soul where men's praise is neither sought nor necessary.

Jesus said: "Blessed are the meek for they shall inherit the earth." The quality of mildness, gentleness and meekness is one which has been admired and advocated in the ethical systems of many religions besides the Christian. As long ago as 600 B.C., Lao-Tse, the Chinese philosopher, said, "The river draws all the rivulets to itself because it puts itself on a lower level, and he who will put himself on the lowest level will draw all the world to him." To take another example, from a completely different culture in another part of the world, the Anglo-Saxon epic poem *Beowulf,* in a passage praising the hero's exploits and character, records, "They said he had been the mildest and gentlest of the kings of the world."

This quality Christ took and brought into connection with God. For the Christian, meekness is not something exercised by a man on his own. It is always held in relation to God, the giver of all good.

Let no one of you be puffed up for one against the other. For who maketh thee to differ from another? And what hast thou that thou didst not receive? Now, if thou didst receive it, why dost thou glory, as if thou hadst not received it?

                                        1 Corinthians 4:6-7

The world often regards mildness as a manifestation of weakness, but in fact it proceeds from strength. The strong, yet personally humble, man can afford to be meek because he has no need to bolster up his ego with the approbation of others. It is the weak and uncertain who need to talk the loudest.

Moses must clearly have been a man of strong personality to achieve what he did. He put heart and courage into a community of slaves, led them out into an unknown but obviously dangerous future, held them together while he disciplined and toughened them, and at last, as he grew old, selected and trained the successor who should take over from him, and lead his people to the goal that he had envisaged forty years before. He must have been one of the greatest leaders of men that the world has ever seen. It is interesting to note what the Hebrew historians recorded as their impression of his character. "The man Moses was very meek, above all the men which were upon the face of the earth." (The Book of Numbers, Chapter 12.)

This quality of meekness displayed by a strong man is seen most clearly of all when we look at our Lord in his arrest and trial. All the time, people are doing things *to* him. He himself seems to do nothing at all but accept what they do. On the surface, he appears entirely passive. Judas comes and kisses him in betrayal. Jesus does not repulse him. The temple guards come to arrest him. Jesus goes with them without any resistance. The members of the Sanhedrin shout accusations against him. Jesus does not reply at all until solemnly bidden to do so "in the Name of the living God." What happens next reveals where the strength lay, and where the weakness. The Sanhedrin was the chief council of the Jewish nation. It was composed of learned, respected, and venerable men. An extraordinary scene now follows. They so far forget their dignity that they crowd round Jesus, even as any vulgar, ill-educated mob would, hitting him and spitting at him. The silent figure standing quietly in the center does not give an impression of weakness. On the contrary, he is the only one present who is acting out of strength, and so can preserve dignity with meekness.

Before Pilate, the situation is the same. On the one hand, there sits the embodiment of Roman power and authority. Pilate is surrounded with all the usual trappings which men use to emphasize their importance. He wears a toga, the mark of Rome; he sits on the judgment seat elevated a few feet above the prisoner; he is flanked by guards and attended by servants; he is clean, rested, and freshly washed and shaved; the prisoner has been awake all night and is weary and sweaty; above all, Pilate has the power of life or death while the prisoner's hands are bound together with ropes as he stands before him for sentencing. And yet, the impression we receive is that it is Jesus, not Pilate, who has control of the situation. The governor is baffled by the complete refusal of the prisoner to make any reply to the charges brought against him. He tries to get him to answer. He sends him out; he calls him back; he tries to pass him over to Herod; he listens to the members of the Sanhedrin, to his wife, to the mob outside. Won't anyone resolve his doubts about what to do? Finally, he calls for a basin and tries to avoid responsibility by washing his hands of the whole affair. There is little doubt who is the stronger figure in this encounter, and yet the strength of Jesus is not shown in argument and self-exculpation. His strength is revealed through meekness and silence.

Blessed, said our Lord, is the man who can act in this way. Not only is he approved of God but he has in fact found one of the secrets for a truly successful human life. Such a man passes through the world calmly, strongly, untroubled by the deceitful anxieties caused by personal pride. The source of his strength and peace is not in himself but in God to whom he has committed himself. "And the rain descended, and the floods came and the winds blew, and beat upon that house; and could not shake it; for it was founded upon a rock."

SCRIPTURE

Lord, I am not high-minded: I have no proud looks.

I do not exercise myself in great matters: which are too high for me.

But I refrain my soul, and keep it low, like as a child that is weaned from his mother; yea, my soul is even as a weaned child.

Psalm 131 :1-2

PRAYER

Take away out of our hearts, O Lord God, all wrong self-confidence and boasting, all high and vain thoughts, all desire to excuse ourselves for our sins or to compare ourselves proudly with others; and grant us rather to take as master and king him who chose to be crowned with thorns and to die in shame for others and for us all, thy Son our Saviour Jesus Christ. Amen.

FROM THE IMITATION OF CHRIST

Is it so hard for you, who are dust and nothingness, to subject yourself to man for God's sake, when I, the Almighty and most high, who created all things from nothing, humbly subjected myself to man for your sake? I became the humblest and least of all men, that you might overcome your pride through my humility (Bk. III, chap. 13).

Is any man made the better for being highly honoured by his fellows? . . . What every man is in your sight, O Lord, that he is and nothing more (Bk. III, chap. 50).

Thomas à Kempis

FROM COMMENTARY ON THE GOSPEL OF ST. JOHN

Why do you make yourself proud, O man? A god has made himself humble for you. You blush perhaps to imitate a humble man; then imitate a humble God.

St. Augustine of Hippo

Chapter 4

ENVY

After Pride, will I speak of the foul sin of Envie, which that is, after the word of the philosopher Aristotle, sorrow at other men's prosperity; and after the word of St. Augustine, it is sorrow at other men's good fortune and joy at other men's harm.

Chaucer, *Canterbury Tales*

The Contrary Virtue to Envy is Brotherly Love

Blessed are the merciful

THE sin of envy consists of discontent because of someone else's good. If I cannot have what you have, then you shall not have it either. It proceeds from self-love coupled with fear. The envious man is made unhappy because in some respect someone else is more fortunate than he. It may be wealth, comfort, happiness, success. Anything that makes him feel inferior may sow the evil seeds of envy in his heart. A man with average brains may envy the first-class intellect of his neighbor. The woman with last season's coat may envy her friend's new furs. An old man may envy the youth of a younger one. The world is full of inequalities of one kind or another. Honors and happiness frequently, in fact, go to the less deserving. Life provides continual occasions for envy in souls who are liable to fall into this corroding sin.

It is bad enough if it remains bottled up inside, for it can wither the spirit and remove all joy and sweetness from life. But all too often, it breeds a dangerous and ugly offspring called jealousy. The root of envy is self-love and discontent at another's good fortune. It very easily leads the soul a step further downward into dislike of the person whose good fortune caused the envy in the first place. In reality, of course, this other person may be quite innocent of offense, but the jealous man cannot see that. As he sees it, that good fortune, that promotion, those good looks, that unexpected legacy, are injuries inflicted upon his own self-love and entitle him to hate his neighbor because of them. So he feels compelled to run him down or deprive him of his happiness. If he is able to do this, he grows warm with a bitter glow of evil satisfaction. As St. Thomas Aquinas pointed out in his *Summa Theologica,* envy is the direct opposite of mercy. The envious man is saddened by his neighbor's prosperity, whereas the merciful man is saddened by his neighbor's misfortune. Hence the envious are not merciful. Their sin leads them easily into cruelty and they quickly learn to derive pleasure from inflicting pain upon the victims of their dislike.

The jealous man cannot keep his hatred to himself but vents it in different ways: by small expressions of dislike (*"I just don't think he's really a nice type of man, that's all"*), by innuendoes and half-truths (*"I happen to know that there are other*

factors involved, but I'm not at liberty to say what they are"),
by imputations of unworthy motives (*"I wonder if that's the
real reason,"* accompanied by a charming and knowing half-
smile, very difficult to resist), by fault-finding (*"She certainly
loused that up—as usual"*), and on into real slander (*"I suppose
you've heard about poor Peg and Charles?"*).

The ruling motive is: there is something about this person,
something he is or something he has, which makes me feel
inferior. I envy him. I am jealous of him. It is not right that
he should be better off (or more popular, or better looking)
than I am. I will try and even things up by doing him what
injury I can. Best of all, I'll take away from him that thing
which makes me feel inferior. If I can't have it, neither shall he.

The well-known fable of "The Dog in the Manger" is an
excellent illustration of this kind of attitude. The horse came
into the stable, tired from a long day's work in the field. The
farmer looked to see that there was a good supply of hay in
the manger, shut him into his stall, and went off to supper. What
the farmer had not noticed was that there was an ill-tempered
little dog lying in the hay. Every time the horse reached up for
a mouthful, the dog snapped at his muzzle and refused to let
him come near. He couldn't eat the hay himself and decided in
his evil little mind that the poor horse should not eat it either.
Envy often drives people to behave in just this kind of way. If
I can't enjoy the pleasure you have, I will do all I can to deprive you of it.

So speaks the character of envy when he makes his appearance
on the stage in Christopher Marlowe's play, *The Tragical History of Dr. Faustus*. He introduces himself with these words:

I am Envy, begotten of a chimney-sweeper and an oyster-wife. I
cannot read, and therefore wish all books were burnt. I am lean
with seeing others eat. O that there would come a famine through all
the world, that all might die and I live alone! Then thou shouldest
see how fat I would be.

Tom Greenwood had been the best woodworker in the small
Vermont town where he had grown up. His grandfather had

designed and masterminded the building of the covered bridge which carried the road from the north over the river and into the town. His father's skill had gone into many a fine house and many a fine barn for miles around. By the time that Tom had grown to be a young man, however, the day for large-scale frame construction in that part of the country was past. His bent, in any case, had always been toward more exact and closer-finished work. He took a delight in the exactly-fitting drawer, the door hung just so, the new leg to the old table perfectly matching the others in style and color. In the years between the two wars, he built up a thriving business, both among the local residents and also, in the summer, among the visitors and tourists who admired the fine workmanship that was evident in all the pieces displayed for sale.

The Japanese attack on Pearl Harbor brought this period of his life to a close. Tom's war took him to Iceland, England, and Italy. He was surprised to find that he quite liked army life. It suited his steady and self-reliant nature. The moments of danger stimulated rather than terrified him. He was able to carry responsibility and to get his way with other men without noise and bluster. He was promoted steadily and, by the time the war ended, had reached the rank of Colonel. He decided to remain in the army on a permanent basis. The pay was good; he had married by this time; and his wife was uncertain that she wanted to live in Vermont. So the years passed. The Korean war gave him a second quick and fierce period of duty in the line. Then, soon afterward, it was time for retirement.

They decided to settle in his home town, and Tom reopened his woodworking business. At first, things went well. People had not forgotten him and an encouraging flow of business came his way. But, after this first bright start, things went less well. His wife, who had been accustomed to the more exciting life on an army base, found Vermont uneventful and dull. Their new social position compared unfavorably with the one they had just relinquished. Worst of all, a new main road was constructed across a fine new steel and concrete bridge about a quarter of a mile downstream from the old covered one. Beside this new road, an Austrian immigrant, Rudi Bitte, opened a store where he sold wooden articles and furniture after the Bavarian manner. He was a skillful craftsman, smiling and hardworking; he was twenty years younger than Tom; above all, his store was on the highway where it caught the eye of the tourists and visitors. He prospered and Tom did not.

As his business declined, Tom took to criticizing the quality of the other man's work; he questioned the motives of those who had decided the location of the new bridge; he muttered darkly about the Government's policy of immigration; he frequently reminded people that the German nation had been responsible for two wars in his lifetime and usually wound up these remarks by some contemptuous reference to Rudi and his heavily accented way of speaking. He fell into a deep enmity toward him which he tried to persuade himself was based upon reason and experience. It was not. It was the fruit of envy and jealousy. When Rudi's mother died back in Vienna and Rudi could not afford to go across to be with his father at the funeral, Tom felt an inward and secret pleasure in the thought of his unhappiness (although he joined outwardly in the general expressions of sympathy). It served Rudi right; he didn't belong there; he never should have come to Vermont in the first place.

Envy is an exceedingly subtle and hidden sin and it is unfortunately often found in the hearts of otherwise good people. It is a sin that often entraps people whom society regards as respectable. There are some people who stand quite firmly against the sins of the flesh, but who seem to find it almost impossible to forgive an injury or to refrain from malicious gossip. And there are people who can resist no sensual temptation, but to whose natures envy and malice seem quite foreign. This lies behind the complaint that religious people are sometimes so much less likable than irreligious, and caused a little girl I once heard of to pray, "O God make all the bad people good, and all the good people nice."

The devil seems to trap religious people in the following way. The greater efforts we make to be good, the more does he suggest that we are better than other people, more wise and more deserving of honor. So we like to find fault with the good deeds of others. The devil whispers that there were ulterior motives

—ambition, self-seeking, desire for praise—and we listen eagerly
because we are envious. It was because of this that the chief
priests and Pharisees could not tolerate Jesus. Pilate, experienced
in dealing with men, perceived quite clearly that it was this
motive which underlay their hostility. "He knew that the chief
priests had delivered him for envy" (Mark 15:10). He was wiser
than they were, a better person, more deserving of honor. They
could not tolerate him. They could not endure him. They delivered him for envy.

There is a story which tells that the devil was once crossing
the African desert. There he found a number of his friends who
were tormenting a holy hermit, who was easily repulsing all
their evil suggestions. The devil called them away and said, "I
will show you what to do." Then, going up to the holy man, he
whispered, "That brother of yours has just been made Bishop
of Alexandria." A scowl of jealousy passed over the hermit's
face. "That is the temptation I would recommend," said the
devil.

In his novel, *The Brothers Karamazov,* Dostoevski gives us a
brilliant study of religious envy at work. Father Zossima was a
monk of great holiness to whom hundreds had come for help
and guidance. After his death, it became apparent that his very
holiness had given rise to envious hatred.

Though the late holy man had won over many hearts, more by
love than by miracles, and had gathered round him a mass of loving
adherents, none the less, in fact rather the more on that account, he
had awakened envy, and so had come to have bitter enemies, secret
and open, not only in the monastery but in the world outside it. He
did no one any harm, but "Why do they think him so saintly?" And
that question alone, continually repeated, gave rise at last to an
intense, insatiable hatred of him. (Part 3, Book VII, Chapter 1.)

We who are church people need to be especially on our guard
against this subtle, disguised, hidden but deadly sin of envy.
"From envy, hatred and malice, and all uncharitableness, Good
Lord deliver us."

The contrary virtue to envy is brotherly love. The second part
of the great Law which our Lord left us is that, after loving

God with every power we possess, we should love our neighbor as ourself. If we truly desire the good of others as much as our own and truly love our neighbors as ourselves (as God requires of us), there will be no room left in our heart for envy. We don't have to start by *liking* everyone (though that may come). Liking people depends upon our emotions and is not always under our control. But we can from the start treat them with Christian love, courtesy, and concern, remembering that a Christian's task in this world is to make himself good and other people happy.

A heart of fire toward God.
A heart of flesh toward others.
A heart of steel toward self.

There was once a monk who took a dislike to one of his companions in the monastery. To begin with, the man spoke with the accent of a country that had long been a traditional enemy of his own native land. Then, living as they were in close daily contact, other things began to be irritating and offensive: the way he ate in the refrectory, the way he sang in the chapel, the work assigned him by the Prior. The first man recognized these feelings of dislike to be wrong and dangerous and set out to fight against them by showing brotherly love. In every way possible, he advanced the other man's interests and showed him marks of kindness and courtesy. When he fell ill, he nursed him with special care. After many years, when both were grown old in the monastery, the second monk drew the first aside one evening and said, "Brother, I have often wondered, what is it about me that you have always liked so much?"

In civilized communities, where actual bodily violence is punishable by law, the desire to hurt, to which envy gives rise, usually finds expression through the tongue. By means of it, people inflict deep and cruel wounds upon each other. "Their teeth are spears and arrows, and their tongue a sharp sword" (Psalm 57). Each of us comes into the world armed with this weapon. To learn the proper control of it is one of the hardest lessons of life. Like all other parts of our body, it was given to us so that we can serve God with it. The proper uses of the tongue are to speak truth and honesty, to say words of comfort, help, and love to other people, and to praise and glorify God.

The harm that can be done by the misuse of the tongue is deep and lasting. One of the worst features of it is that, once the harm is done, it is usually almost impossible to undo it. The magicians of the ancient world understood this when they uttered their charms. They perceived that when a word is spoken, a deed is done. Something has happened that cannot be recalled. So it is with us. How often we may regret something we have said and wish to unsay it. But very often this cannot be done. The apology, the correction, or the denial rarely catches up completely with the original assertion.

There is a story told of St. Francis of Assisi. One day a woman came to him and confessed that she had been guilty of malicious gossip. She asked how she might find forgiveness. St. Francis told her to pluck a goose and to lay one feather on the doorstep of each person about whom she had said malicious things. The woman went away and did as he had said. Then she returned to the saint and asked what she should do next. He sent her on the rounds once more and told her to gather the feathers up again. Of course, by this time, they had flown all over the village. St. Francis said to her, "You may wish to repent, and that is good. But you can never recall the words that you have spoken. They have gone on their way doing harm. You have committed a sin for which no reparation is possible. Confess your sin to Almighty God, and ask for his forgiveness, for he is the only one who can forgive you."

Some years ago, there used to be a group of figures that were often to be seen above the fireplaces in people's homes. They were three monkeys sitting side by side. One had his hands over his eyes, another over his ears, and the third over his mouth. They were supposed to remind all who saw them that it was best to see no evil, to hear no evil, and to speak no evil. There are fewer fireplaces in homes these days and so perhaps that is why we do not seem to see these wise monkeys as often as we used to do. But their advice is just as worth heeding today as ever it was.

The temper of mind of this age is impatient of such restraints, indeed it regards them as unvirile or even as dishonest. But I am not pleading for dishonesty or cowardice. It is sometimes necessary to speak up and to wound; however, such times do not occur as frequently as most people like to think. A good rule is never to report something that may hurt someone else unless a still greater hurt to others will result from concealing it. In the old samplers, on which children of an earlier century used to work, learning embroidery and moral maxims at the same time, I have sometimes read: "Speak not till thou hast questioned, Is it wise? Is it kind? Is it true?" Checks like these upon the tongue help to establish a mastery over it. We will be wise not to think ourselves too superior to need them or to benefit from them. It will perhaps sometimes mean that we shall sit silent while others are enjoying a time of malicious gossip. It will perhaps mean the sacrificing of a witty remark which would have earned us a laugh and a feeling of clever worldliness. We shall sometimes appear rather more stupid than we really are and be regarded by our friends as slow and dull company. But, as someone once remarked, it is better to keep one's mouth shut and be thought a fool, than to open it and remove all doubt (at least, in God's eyes). The evil wrought by the tongue is so disruptive and destructive that it is worth paying a small price like this in order to avoid contributing our share to it.

Curse the whisperer and double-tongued: for such have destroyed many that were at peace. A backbiting tongue hath disquieted many . . . strong cities hath it pulled down, and overthrown the houses of great men. A backbiting tongue hath cast out virtuous women . . . The stroke of the whip maketh marks in the flesh; but the stroke of the tongue breaketh the bones. Many have fallen by the edge of the sword; but not so many as have fallen by the tongue.

Ecclesiasticus

There is another very good rule to follow whenever we find ourselves slipping into jealousy or malice. This is always to look for a commendable reason for someone's action, always to place the best possible construction on what he did or said. Envy and jealousy prompt us to look immediately for some bad or discreditable motive. But it is usually possible to think of good ones, if we try, and the very act of looking for good motives often removes the weed planted in our heart by envious evil imputation, before it has time to take root.

Perhaps the best weapon of all is to pray for the person about whom we are tempted to feel bitter or jealous. Hold him up before God for his blessing upon him in every way he needs. Pray that God may give him good health and happiness all the days of his life and bring him to everlasting happiness in heaven. This is of course what God wants for him. By praying for these things yourself, you are putting yourself on God's side; you are beginning to look at the person as God looks at him. You will find that prayers like this will be blessed to you too, by sweetening the sour infection of malice or envy that had crept into your heart. Before you know it, you may end up by quite liking the fellow after all.

Trust in God's care is a real defense for us against envy of what may appear to be the unfair good fortune of someone else. God loves equally every soul that he has created and he "divideth to every man severally as he will" (1 Corinthians 12:11). What is best for one is not necessarily best for another. What seem to us great advantages often carry with them great temptations and responsibilities; and not all souls are able to face these successfully. Positions of power tend to corrupt those who hold them; beautiful women may find themselves being tempted to vanity or lust in ways which homely ones escape through their very homeliness; our Lord warned us that rich people find their way into the kingdom with much greater difficulty than the poor. If we cultivate a thankful heart, we come to understand how real are our own blessings and to live gratefully and happily with them. How foolish to spoil the happiness we have through envy of the happiness enjoyed by someone else. My good is in no way lessened by what appears to me to be the greater good of another person. In the words of the cockney cab driver, "Life may not be all you'ld like; but it's all you 'ave. So 'ave it. Stick a geranium in your 'at and be 'appy."

Those things in life which tend to lower our self-esteem are not losses but instruments of good. They can save us from conceit and self-sufficiency. They can teach us kindness and humility. Their discipline can lead us to the gates of heaven.

"Blessed are the merciful," said Jesus, "for they shall obtain mercy." This lovely virtue is the exact opposite of envy. The envious man enjoys the misfortunes of others and indulges his cruelty by adding to them if he can. The merciful man is made sad by the sadness of others and does whatever he can to relieve it.

Our Lord used no more characteristic expression to describe his own spiritual position than when he said: "Go ye and learn what this means, I desire mercy and not sacrifice." He deals with us not according to our deserts but according to our need for mercy.

The Law of Moses and the righteousness of Judaism were both directed toward mercy. The seat of God himself in the Tabernacle was called the "mercy seat." A conception of the compassion and the loving-kindness of God, and of men's consequent duty to show these qualities to their fellow men, reached deep into the heart of the Israelite religion. And yet, by the time of Jesus, both righteousness and the law had come too often in fact to stand for the opposite. The law had come to mean the letter of the law and not its spirit. Unmerciful men were able to cloak their sin with an outward show of the law's observance. Righteousness had degenerated into the scrupulous keeping of outward ritual forms that had, in many hearts, killed the very life of the spirit which they were intended to foster. So lip service was paid to the ideal of mercy, but in many cases the reality was lacking. But mercy calls for more than lip service. To mouth appropriate words or to indulge in sentimental dreamings on the subject is not to be merciful. Mercy becomes real only in action, only in the doing of concrete acts of mercy.

In Dostoevski's unforgettable novel, *The Brothers Karamazov,* on one occasion Lise's mother comes to see Father Zossima. She is described as being a sentimental society lady of genuinely good disposition in many respects. She pours out a great deal of enthusiastic but unrealistic talk to the monk. She is caught up

in luxurious feelings of compassion and is enjoying them senti-
mentally for their own sake. "I so love humanity that I often
dream of forsaking all that I have, leaving Lise, and becoming
a sister of mercy. I close my eyes and think and dream, and at
that moment I feel full of strength to overcome all obstacles.
No wounds, no festering sores could at that moment frighten
me. I would bind them up and wash them with my own hands. I
would nurse the afflicted. I would be ready to kiss such wounds."
She carries on in this way for a long time and the monk listens
patiently. At last, when she has finished, he remarks gently
but with a certain dry irony, "It is much, my daughter, and it
is well, that your mind is full of these dreams and not others.
Sometimes, unawares, you may do a good deed in reality."
Mercy is existential. It becomes real only in action.

The opposition that our Lord encountered was not so much
from the formality and spiritual deadness that prevailed as from
something much more serious which underlay them. There was
an almost total absence of sympathy, pity, and compassion. The
Pharisees did not care that a crippled man had been made
whole, but only that the ritual law of the Sabbath had been
broken. Yet sympathy and compassion are the things that fill
and make human life. Without them, we become hard and de-
humanized. Even a polite form of words, spoken without love,
can be turned into a cruel insult. Without mercy and love, the
observance of righteousness and the law are sterile and empty;
but where they are present, human encounters can be trans-
formed. A wise man once said: "Where there is no love, put
love, and you will extract love." This calling-out of love by the
giving first of one's own love, even to the unloving and the unlovely, is the very work which Christ himself did among us. It
brings his blessing in return. "Blessed are the merciful," he
said, "for they shall obtain mercy."

SCRIPTURE

Charity suffereth long, and is kind; charity envieth not;
charity vaunteth not itself, is not puffed up, doth not behave
itself unseemly, seeketh not her own, is not easily provoked,
thinketh no evil; rejoiceth not in iniquity, but rejoiceth in the

truth; beareth all things, believeth all things, hopeth all things, endureth all things.

I Corinthians 13:4-7

Let all bitterness, and wrath, and anger, and clamour, and evil-speaking, be put away from you, with all malice.

And be ye kind one to another, tenderhearted, forgiving one another, even as God for Christ's sake hath forgiven you.

Ephesians 4:31-32

PRAYERS

Grant, O Lord, that as we remember the kindnesses which we have received and never merited, and the punishments which we have deserved and never suffered, we may give thanks to thee for thine unfailing mercies and for the mercies of our fellow men, through Jesus Christ our Lord. Amen.

O God, the First and the Last, the Beginning and the End: Thou who wast with us in our birth, be with us through our life; thou who art with us through life, be with us at our death; and, because thy mercy will not leave us then, grant us to rise to the life everlasting with thee, who livest and reignest God for ever and ever. Amen.

Set a watch, O Lord, upon our tongue:
that we may never speak the cruel word which is untrue;
or, being true, is not the whole truth;
or, being wholly true, is merciless. Amen.

A SEVENTEENTH-CENTURY PRAYER

O that my eyes might closed be
To what concerns me not to see;
That deafness might possess mine ear
To what concerns me not to hear;
That truth my tongue might always tie
From ever speaking foolishly;
That no vain thought might ever rest
Or be conceived within my breast;
That by each deed and word and thought

Glory may to my God be brought.
But what are wishes! Lord, mine eye
On thee is fixed; to thee I cry!
Wash Lord and purify my heart,
And make it clean in every part;
And when 'tis clean, Lord, keep it too
For this is more than I can do.

                    Thomas Elwood, 1639 A.D.

Chapter 5

ANGER

This sin of Anger, after the definition of Saint Augustine, is wicked will to be avenged by word or dede. Anger is the fervent blood of man quickened in his heart, through which he wisheth harme to him that he hateth.

Chaucer, *Canterbury Tales*

The Contrary Virtue to Anger is Patience

Blessed are the peacemakers

THE sin of anger has its roots in instinct and passion. It is a natural reaction from something that thwarts us. This leads some people to think that they cannot help being angry. They were born (they tell us) with a naturally impatient and hasty temper, and so they cannot help it when it gets the better of them. There is a common tendency to personify anger as if it were some kind of external influence. We hear such expressions as, "My temper overcame me," or, "Rage took possession of him." Although there is an element of truth lying behind these ways of speaking of anger, this tendency to personify it is really an attempt to retain our self-respect by putting the blame somewhere else. To speak of our anger in this way is to dissociate ourselves from it, to represent it as something abnormal, external, not really belonging to ourselves.

It is significant that we like to speak of our vices in this way but that we regard our virtues as something of our own. If a person acts in a dishonest manner, he prefers to describe it afterward (if he is found out) as the result of an external force beyond his control. "I was overcome by temptation," he explains. It was not really I myself who was to blame. It was the result of an external force beyond my control. But if he acts honestly, that is something else again. This time, it resulted from his own true character. "I was too honest to do such a thing," he reports with manly simplicity. This was not the result of anything external. This was himself acting naturally.

We all tend to personify our temptations or defects in this way. "I gave way to evil thoughts." "My pride got the better of me." These, and similar expressions not difficult to recognize, are an attempt to retain our own self-respect and to extenuate our lapses in the eyes of others. Our failures are represented as being due to forces outside ourselves. The onset of these forces was both too sudden and too severe for us to be expected to have resisted them. We were not really to blame. This is a rather dangerous and self-deceptive habit to fall into. In reality, of course, it is the man himself who thought the evil thoughts, or who was angry, proud, or dishonest. Any way of speaking that disguises this unwelcome fact from him is a step backward spiritually. We all naturally think far too well of ourselves in

64

any case. It is not good to be habitually adding to this inborn self-conceit by little dishonest tricks of this kind.

It is true that some people have naturally quick tempers which often land them into trouble before they know where they are. But it is not true that they can do nothing about it or that there is no more to be said. Such people are weak in this particular respect as other people are weak in different ways. We all have our personal weaknesses against which we have to fight. We are all born weak in some aspect or another of our character and God expects us to overcome whatever our special weakness may be. The person who is handicapped by a quick temper must fight with his weakness like everyone else. It is no excuse to say that he was born with it.

The preliminary stage of anger is impatience. Something thwarts us, and an angry impatience is the natural and instinctive reaction. Joe Slater lived several miles out of town in a new suburb built on what used to be a large farm property. Mary and he had decided that it would be better for the children to grow up in those clean and pleasant surroundings rather than in the somewhat rundown neighborhood where they had settled immediately after their marriage, and which had been all that Joe could afford in those days. He was happy about the move. The only drawback so far as he was concerned was the rather long daily drive to work. He was not yet sufficiently senior to rate his own parking place at the office, and the difficulty in finding somewhere to leave his car during the day was a source of continual irritation. One day, he noticed a space behind the paint store in the factory yard, which would be just right. He cleared away a few old drums and cans and adopted the space as his own. Relieved of the need to compete for space in the street, he was able to leave home nearly fifteen minutes later than before. He was pleased that this little problem had been happily solved. Then, one morning, as he swung easily round the corner of the paint store, there was someone else's car calmly parked in his private, secret place. There was nothing to do but to drive out of the yard again and to look for a parking space in the streets. By this time, all those spaces near the factory were taken. He had to drive round for some time before he finally found a place nearly a mile away. He reached his office twenty minutes late in a state of angry impatience.

Later that day, back at their home, Mary had been baking a cake. She had taken a great deal of trouble with it. It was to be her contribution to the home-cooking stall at the church sale the next day. She usually baked her cake for this event several days beforehand, but this year, because of one thing and another, she had been obliged to leave it rather late. She had a well-deserved reputation as a cook, and it was important to her that this year's cake should continue to sustain it. It was to be a light sponge cake with special effects of icing and decoration to be added afterward. At last, it was safely in the oven and was rising nicely. Mary went into the laundry to catch up on her ironing. This was the moment when her neighbor's five-year-old chose to come across to visit her, to open the screen door, look inside the kitchen, see no one, let the door slam smartly back and depart, leaving behind him the ruin of an hour's work. We can pass over a detailed account of Mary's reaction, except to say that it would provide us with an excellent example of this first, simple, and instinctive phase of anger. Whenever our convenience, our comfort, our plans, or our prestige are thwarted in some way, the instinctive reaction is an immediate feeling of angry impatience or irritation.

This first stage of the sin can easily and quickly be extended into a mood of anger. Now the emotions have become involved. The person has passed into a state of wrath where things that would not normally irritate him become occasions for further outbursts of bad temper. When Joe Slater at last found a parking place for his car, someone passing by on the sidewalk jogged his elbow as he was locking the door, so that he dropped his keys into the gutter. Normally he would have smilingly accepted the other man's apology but now, because he had passed into an emotional state of anger, he turned on him with "Look where you're going, you clumsy oaf." When he reached his office, he tried his secretary's patience pretty severely on several occasions by minor fault-finding and general grumpiness. It was not until an hour or so had elapsed that he had recovered his usual good humor.

After her impatience at the ruination of her cake, Mary also allowed herself to pass into an angry mood. Her children, arriving home from school shortly afterward, quickly learned that today was not a day when small offenses would be regarded indulgently. Michael's muddy shoes, Pamela's running nose, and Janet's slamming of the door each in turn provoked an impatient rebuke from their mother. Wise from past experiences of the incalculable ways of adult behavior, without another word being spoken the children instinctively understood that the sooner they went out again to play the better for all concerned. Fortunately, another two hours were to pass before Joe reached home. By this time, both husband and wife had had time to recover from their angry moods and were able to meet each other with sweetness and affection. But, being both naturally quick tempered, they were not always so lucky.

Anger is like an infection. A person becomes angry. He says harsh words, he wounds, he offends, he tries the patience of those around him so that they in turn begin to feel angry as a result. If this happens, we now have two or three more people angry where there had been at first only one. The infection has spread. As a result of the irritation over losing his parking place, Joe Slater was in a carping and complaining mood. He brusquely returned three letters to his secretary for retyping, because of one or two small errors that he would normally have simply corrected with his pen. Offended by his sharp manner, she withdrew to the outer office and set about the retyping with no good grace. A salesman who arrived at that moment received a sour look and a quick dismissal, and was sent off to his next call depressed and irritated in his turn. In the matter of a few minutes, the infection of Joe's anger had spread to two other people as well.

A third and worse stage of anger sometimes follows. The sin becomes much more serious if we deliberately continue in the state of anger. The mind as well as the emotions have now gone over to the enemy. The result is a brooding condition of evil temper in which the mind deliberately encourages and prolongs the anger and takes a kind of dark and twisted satisfaction in it. Robert Burns had a true glimpse of this condition when, in his poem "Tam o'Shanter," he described the woman waiting for her husband to come home from the inn as "nursing her wrath to keep it warm." The phrase expresses it exactly. The person broods over real or fancied injuries; he exaggerates to himself the bad qualities (or what he thinks are the bad qualities) of the person with whom he is angry; he deliberately encourages and prolongs the mood of resentment. He probably gives himself over to plotting revenge, or at least to desiring revenge and savoring it in his mind. He plans bitter things to say and do. Such a sulky, sullen, black temper is very unpleasant and its degree of deliberateness makes it a serious sin. The will has chosen to remain in a state of anger and to fan its flames.

The depths of anger are reached if the soul passes into passion in which there is complete loss of self-control. The victim of the sin in this extreme form looks as if he has become temporarily insane. "Rage took possession of him," we say. Or, "He was beside himself with anger." The face flushes, the voice rises to a shout, the body sweats, the power of reason is temporarily overthrown. The person indeed looks as if he has become less than human for the time being. Such rage is doubly dangerous because it may find expression not only in violent words but in violent deeds. Passion of this kind shakes the soul to its foundations. Whole battalions of sins rush in to destroy that inner peace of soul which is the essential condition of keeping close to God. When the passion subsides, the soul is left weary and empty, often at the mercy of any temptation that may come along. Many a man has not realized what diabolical possibilities there are within him until he has caught sight of himself in a fit of passion. Fortunately, it does sometimes occur that a person is able to see himself, as it were from outside, at such a moment. To do so is a disturbing experience for anyone. The soul has very obviously gone over to the enemy and been very clearly overwhelmed by the forces of darkness and evil.

Now what can we do against the sin of anger? In the first place, we should never prolong or encourage the state once we have fallen into it. A quick apology will usually heal the breach which our anger has caused and end the matter right there. It takes a real degree of humility and often courage to make up a quarrel quickly, but that is the way and time to do it.

> A little explained,
> A little endured,
> A little forgiven,
> And the quarrel is cured.

How many family quarrels and estrangements that have lasted for generations among those who should live in brotherly love and concord were due in the first instance to nothing more than sullen anger and pride that would not repent?

Miss Euphemia Branscome and Miss Sophy Branscombe have not spoken to each other for years. They are sisters and live in the same town; but they hold no communication the one with the other. Years ago, after their parents died, they used to live contentedly, together with their younger brother Timothy, in the family home on Main Street. Eventually, Timothy was married and Euphemia was asked to be a bridesmaid but Sophy was not. The fact that she had not previously been closely acquainted with the bride was a factor which seemed to Sophy to be of little importance compared with the slight that she felt she had received.

Euphemia had looked extremely handsome at the wedding and several people had commented upon it in Sophy's hearing. Euphemia had been conscious of it too and had dropped a few less-than-tactful remarks of her own in the same vein. Sophy attended the wedding and the reception in an atmosphere of careful and cold politeness.

When the couple returned from the honeymoon, there had been a housewarming at their new apartment but she had declined the invitation, insisting that only what she referred to as "the principals" at the wedding should attend. What she really hoped for was a little affectionate urging to be present and, if this had been forthcoming, nothing would have kept her away. But it was not. The others felt that if Sophy wanted to behave like a child, that was her concern. But no one put anything of this into words. Sophy's refusal was outwardly accepted at its face value and the breach deepened.

Not long after this, the sisters decided to sell the old large family home, and each moved into a separate apartment. At Thanksgiving, Sophy invited her brother and his wife to dinner, but not Euphemia. Timothy and his wife accepted, expecting that Euphemia was of course to be there too. When they found that she had not been invited, they tried to persuade Sophy to include her. But she was adamant. She herself had not felt it right to come to their housewarming, she explained, but now the least she could do was to entertain dear Timothy and Sarah in her own small establishment. Anxious to maintain good relations with her, they went. Euphemia was hurt, as Sophy intended she should be, and passed her sister by without any greeting when they chanced to meet on the steps of the post office the next morning. Maintaining within herself the pretense of having acted with complete correctness, Sophy in her turn chose to be angered by her sister's slight and resolved to return it with interest when opportunity offered.

Further opportunities certainly did occur on both sides and the sisters drifted into positions of hostility from which neither would move. They gradually entered into different circles of friends, acquired different interests and, as the years passed, became in fact strangers to each other. Neither really knew anything about the person that the other had now become.

So they passed through middle age into lonely old age, separated and estranged. They had long forgotten that the whole unhappy business could have been prevented by one simple quick loving apology at that far-off wedding reception fifty years ago.

It takes a real degree of humility and often courage to make up a quarrel quickly, but that is the way and the time to do it. Once we have allowed ourselves to fall into a state of anger, we should never allow ourselves to commit the further sin of prolonging and encouraging it. "Let not the sun go down upon your wrath," wrote St. Paul. "Agree with thine adversary quickly, whiles thou art in the way with him," said Jesus. "If thou bring thy gift to the altar, and there rememberest that thy brother hath ought against thee; leave there thy gift before the altar, and go thy way. First be reconciled to thy brother, and then come and offer thy gift."

God is Love itself and so hatred and anger must always be repugnant to him. The words of the Invitation in the service of Holy Communion in the Anglican Church remind us that one of the essential preparations for coming to receive our Lord in the Sacrament of his Body and Blood is that we purge our hearts of anger and resentment. "Ye that do truly and earnestly repent you of your sins and are in love and charity with your neighbors . . . draw near with faith and take this holy Sacrament." St. John in his first letters reminds us of the same fundamental truth that our love for God must express itself in love for our fellow men also.

Beloved, let us love one another: for love is of God, and every one that loveth is born of God and knoweth God. He that loveth not, knoweth not God; for God is love . . . If a man say, I love God, and hateth his brother, he is a liar. For he that loveth not his brother whom he hath seen, how can he love God whom he hath not seen? And this commandment have we from him, That he who loveth God love his brother also.

I John 4:7-8, 20-21

If someone has done us an injury, we have never fully recovered from it until we have forgiven him. As long as our resentment at the injury still rankles in our heart, it still has power over us for evil. We are not free of it until in the deep, secret recesses of our heart we have forgiven. For our own sake, as much as for the other person's, this must be done. Only then is the incident really closed so far as we are concerned. Only then can our heart enter into peace and quietness. Forgiveness is the price required for our own peace of soul.

Not all anger is wrong. Our Lord was sometimes angry and there certainly is such a thing as "righteous indignation." But only the truly humble man can be angry without sinning. This is because with him the personal element is eliminated. The reason for his anger is not because he has been hurt or because his pride has been wounded. The anger of the humble man alone has moral force because he is angered not for himself but for something beyond himself. Our Lord's anger was like this. This was why the cattle drovers and moneychangers in the Temple courtyard cringed before him. Physically, they were just as strong as he was, and there were many of them. They could easily have prevented his overturning the tables and driving out the cattle, if physical force had been all that was required. But it was the moral force of the anger of a humble and selfless personality that drove them out. A small improvised whip of cords in the hand of one man would not have been sufficient by itself.

It is this moral force which lies behind the seemingly paradoxical phrase "the wrath of the Lamb." Our Lord is called "the Lamb of God" chiefly because he is the perfect offering for the sins of the whole world, but also because his patient humility in suffering was like that of a lamb. But meekness does not mean weakness. When the humble Lamb is angered, who may stand against such anger as that?

And the stars of heaven fell into the earth, even as a fig tree casteth her untimely figs, when she is shaken of a mighty wind. And the heaven departed as a scroll when it is rolled together; and every mountain and island were moved out of their places. And the kings of the earth, and the great men, and the rich men, and the chief captains, and the mighty men, and every bondman, and every free man, hid themselves in the dens and in the rocks of the mountains; and said to the mountains and rocks, Fall on us, and hide us from the face of him that sitteth on the throne, and from the wrath of the Lamb.

Revelation 6:13-16

There certainly is such a thing as "righteous wrath" but few of us are justified in claiming this flattering description for our own moments of bad temper, for we lack the humility to "be angry and sin not."

> *Thou* to wax fierce
>   In the cause of the Lord.
> To threat and to pierce
>   With the heavenly sword;

Anger and zeal
And the joy of the brave
Who bade *thee* to feel?
Sin's slave?

It is a dangerous thing for most of us to start seeing ourselves in the role of Michael the Archangel. Our anger has too much of our personal pride and interest mixed up in it. Too often what people like to think is "righteous indignation" is only an attempt to have the best of both worlds: they want to enjoy losing their temper without being ashamed of themselves at the time or sorry for it afterwards. In his book *Babbitt,* that sharply etched study of small-town life, Sinclair Lewis drew a penetrating picture of this false kind of "righteous indignation," in Zilla, Paul Riesling's scolding wife.

Zilla's face was wrinkled like the Medusa, her voice was a dagger of corroded brass. She was full of the joy of righteousness and bad temper. She was a crusader, and, like all crusaders, she exulted in the opportunity to be vicious in the name of virtue.

The contrary virtue to anger is patience. This is not a very popular or admired quality these days. We are encouraged to admire the man who has a blazing row, stands up for himself and gets his rights. The fact that we tend to think well of such a man is a measure of the pagan spirit of the age. The example of Christ was quite the opposite, who "when he was reviled, reviled not again; when he suffered, he threatened not." It takes a very strong man to be patient in this kind of way.

Patience is essentially a Christian virtue. The word scarcely appears in the Old Testament, but the New Testament is full of it. "Bring forth fruit with patience," said our Lord, and, "In patience, ye shall win your souls."

One helpful method of acquiring this virtue is to make a deliberate act of acceptance of each irritation as it comes. The parking place is found to be unexpectedly occupied, the sponge cake is ruined by a thoughtless child, and a quick half-second prayer rises to meet the irritation. "O God, this has come my way. I will accept it." In this way, we are united for a quick moment with the will of God, and we can be on the road to forming a habit of patience. I have known some people who have so learned this lesson that they have acquired deep wells of patience which keep them cool and refreshed throughout the day.

There is a pagan ideal of self-control which looks something like the Christian but is not really the same at all. The ancient Romans (they have their modern counterparts) aimed at the ideal of an austere man striving for mastery of himself and producing a strong ego. A hard, proud, but not ignoble kind of man. The Christian ideal is directed toward a different end, toward the fulfillment of the will of God in us. It is not simply the producing of a strong ego but the allowing God to bring his order into the Christian character. The aim is not to produce self-control but God's control.

If you are aware of the sin of anger in your makeup, patience is the virtue to strive for. It may be had by increasingly allowing God to control our reaction to the annoyances we meet, whether from things or people, as we travel along the little journey of each day.

"Blessed are the peacemakers," said Jesus, "for they shall be called the children of God." Peace has been something that men have longed for, in all ages. They have always instinctively felt that hatred, anger, and war are not the best of which humanity is capable. During the Old Testament years, men looked forward to the day when the Messiah should come and this hope of his coming was bound up with another one: that he would bring peace with him. One of his titles was "The Prince of Peace" and this was to be one of the characteristic and fundamental features of his reign.

And he shall judge among many people, and rebuke strong nations afar off; and they shall beat their swords into plowshares, and their spears into pruning hooks; nation shall not lift up a sword against nation, neither shall they learn war any more. But they shall sit every man under his vine and under his fig tree; and none shall make them afraid.

Micah 4:3-4

When the Messiah came, this peace was to extend even to the natural world, where the preying by one creature upon another is a sign and symptom that God's plan for his creation has been twisted and defaced. The coming of the Messiah was to bring peace in these areas also.

The wolf also shall dwell with the lamb, and the leopard shall lie down with the kid; and the calf and the young lion and the fatling together; and a little child shall lead them.

Isaiah 11:6

When in fact he came, though it was not in the way men looked for, it was with this very message that his birth was heralded. "Glory to God in the highest," sang the angels, "and on earth, Peace." It became one of his favorite words. "Go in peace" he was constantly saying to those to whom he had brought healing and forgiveness. It was the greeting which he told his disciples to give when he sent them to visit through the country-side in his name. As they entered any house, they were to say: "Peace be to this house."

This same message is that which the Church must still give to a world where men are separated from each other by hatred and anger. Christ reconciled men to God. In him, Christians must show men how to become reconciled to each other. In Christ, the three great divides of humanity are transcended: race, class, and sex. ("There is neither Jew nor Greek, there is neither bond nor free, there is neither male nor female; for ye are all one in Christ Jesus.") It is, of course, only too easy to point to places where the Church has failed to bring recon-ciliation and peace in these ways. The failures leap to the mind, but they do so because they are exceptions. It cannot be denied that the Church has in fact brought people of different races to love one another more successfully than has any other society; that in the body of the Church different social classes are in fact able to meet on common ground more easily and more naturally than they could anywhere else; and that not only has Christianity been the chief historical instrument of the emancipation of women, but in the Church, and above all in a Christian family, the two sexes have learned to find that mutual fulfillment that was the will of God for them from the beginning.

To bring peace where there was anger and variance is to do

the work of God. The Christian is not to take the line of least resistance, nor the course of immediate expediency; but the person who can "make men to be of one mind in a house" is one whom our Lord calls blessed. Some people are able to be spiritual catalysts. They are the means by which others can live together in harmony.

The story of Miss Euphemia and Miss Sophy Branscombe earlier in this chapter might have ended quite differently if there had been a peacemaker as a go-between. If there had been someone who cared enough for them both to take the trouble, and who had resources of tact and good humor, such a person could have repaired the breach before it had become too wide. To act in such a way is to do the work of God, who will not withhold his recognition, for those who do these things shall be called his children.

It was not even necessary that a third person should bring about the reconciliation of the two sisters. Either of them could have done it herself. All that was needed was that the desire to be a peacemaker should have been stronger than the desire to pamper to a wounded self-esteem. That was all that was needed but, as human beings are constituted, how much that is! To be the first to reach out in loving apology is not easy. It is to die a little. It is to have some share in that death to self that is the very means by which we may be united to our Lord in crucifixion and so pass with him into the new life of resurrection. Our Lord tells us that such people are truly happy for God shall call them his children.

PRAYER

Give us, O Lord, the grace to be patient as thou wast patient; that we may gently bear with the faults of others, and strive at all times to root out our own.

A PRAYER OF ST. FRANCIS OF ASSISI

O Lord, make me an instrument of thy peace. Where there is hatred, let me sow love; where there is injury, pardon; where there is doubt, faith; where there is despair, hope; where there is darkness, light; where there is sadness, joy.

Grant that I may not so much seek to be consoled as to console; not so much to be understood as to understand; not so much to be loved as to love; for it is in giving that we receive; it is in pardoning that we are pardoned; and it is in dying that we are born to eternal life.

The Book of Proverbs, 16:32.
The Book of Isaiah, 53:5-7.
The First Epistle of Saint Peter, 2:19-23.
The Epistle of Saint James, 1:19-20.

FROM THE IMITATION OF CHRIST

It is no great matter to associate with the good and gentle for this is naturally pleasant to everyone. All men are glad to live at peace, and prefer those who are of their own way of thinking. But to be able to live at peace among hard, obstinate, and undisciplined people and those who oppose us, is a great grace, and a most commendable and manly achievement. (Book II, Chapter 3.)

Do not say, "I cannot endure such things from this person," or, "I will not tolerate these things: he has done me great injury, and accused me of things I never considered; from another person I might bear it, and regard it as something that must be endured." Such thoughts are foolish, for you ignore the merit of patience and him who rewards it, and think only of the person who has injured you and the wrong you endure.

You are not truly patient if you will only endure what you think fit, and only from those whom you like. A truly patient man does not consider by whom he is tried, whether by his superior, his equal, or his inferior; whether by a good and holy man, or by a perverse and wicked person.

Always be ready for battle if you wish for victory; you cannot win the crown of patience without a struggle: if you refuse to suffer, you refuse the crown. Therefore, if you desire the crown, fight manfully and endure patiently. Without labor, no rest is won; without battle, there can be no victory. (Bk. III, chap. 19.)

Thomas à Kempis

Chapter 6

SLOTH (OR ACCIDIE)

After the sinne of Wrath, now will I speke of the sinne of Accidie, or slouth: for Enview blindeth the heart of a man, and he troubleth a man, and Accidie maketh him heavy, gloomy and peevish.

. . . And Saint Augustine saith: It is sadness at goodness and sadness at harm . . . He doth all things with sadness, and with peevishness, slackness and excusation, with idleness and without good will.

Chaucer, *Canterbury Tales*

The Contrary Virtue to Sloth is Diligence

Blessed are they that mourn

THE sin with which this chapter is concerned is difficult to define because it takes so many different forms. It is very much more than mere laziness, though that is one of its manifestations; and, for that reason, the modern English title of sloth for this sin is a little misleading. The technical name for it is *accidie*.

It is the gloom of those who ought not to be sad, who willfully allow a morbid somberness to settle down upon them. It is a mood that makes a man unable to greet with his usual courtesy and pleasure even the coming of close and valued friends. It is a condition of the soul which severs a man from thoughts of God. Everything seems to have become annoying, stale, and unnecessary. *Accidie* is a kind of sorrowful despondency, a listlessness, a tepid lukewarm condition wherein the soul gives itself up to a fruitless, hopeless, joyless, and yet restless indolence. There seems to be a sullen, heavy, dreary mist about the heart, chilling it and darkening it. It is the mood of days on which it seems that we cannot laugh genuinely, and when we cannot get rid of a dull or acrid tone in the voice.

In his *Inferno* (VII, 121-124), Dante gives us a tremendous and relentless picture of the results of giving way to this willful gloom which in the end shuts out all light and love from life. "Sullen were we in the sweet air, that is gladdened by the sun, carrying lazy smoke within our hearts; now we lie sullen here in the back mire."

Accidie leads to a negation of life with all its splendors and challenges. The man who is caught in its insidious toils exaggerates the difficulties that lie between him and any high attainments. He measures the weight of all tasks by his own disinclination for them. He makes use of any easy excuse that comes to hand. The writer of the Book of Proverbs hit this off nicely. The lazy man wants an excuse—any excuse—to postpone going out to work. It doesn't matter how impossible and far-fetched the excuse may be, only so long as it is something he can use to postpone action.

The slothful man saith, there is a lion in the way; a lion is in the streets. As the door turneth upon its hinges, so doth the slothful upon his bed . . . The sluggard is wiser in his own conceit than seven men that can render a reason.

Proverbs 26:13-14, 16

All noble things require a certain hardness in the achieving of them. The slothful man exaggerates this hardness in his imagination until it approaches nearer and nearer to impossibility. He settles down into a lazy contentment with low aims and low attainments. When challenged to real effort, he quickly becomes resentful and irritated. Churchmen who undertake the work of canvassing their fellow parishioners to pledge in support of their church run into the reaction sometimes. A man who has become accustomed to a low level of giving, is outraged and scandalized by the suggestion that he should give a tenth of his income. It seems fantastic and impossible to him. The very idea is altogether too painful to contemplate. It is quite inadmissible. He explodes into angry accusations against the church that has ventured to make such an indecorous suggestion to him. *Accidie* has sapped away his ability to respond.

People who "enjoy bad health" are another example of this many-sided sin. We all know them. They are familiar figures in doctors' offices, on psychiatrists' couches, and in priests' studies. Perhaps some genuine ailment is there at the bottom, but upon it has been erected a monstrous superstructure of complaint, self-pity, and withdrawal from life and action. What such people are looking for is sympathy. But sympathy only reinforces their sin. The only thing that will really help them, if by God's grace they are able to receive it, is encouragement to leave the easy downward path of *accidie* and to begin the unwelcome climb up toward responsible living. This is a hard and unattractive path but, if they can be brought to understand what it is they have been doing, they may be helped to make their way back to the happy wholesomeness which is God's will for us all. The Church's words for this are repentance, forgiveness, and restoration.

Chester was a teller in a bank. His father had been a crane operator for one of the local contractors, but Chester had completed high school and both his parents had felt that it would be a waste of his education for him to go in for manual work of that kind. Chester himself had had no strong feelings about the matter. He had not enjoyed his school work particularly, nor had he wanted to drive a crane.

During the last six months before graduation, booklets about various kinds of work were made available to the students. Chester read them without much interest. But the one on "Banking as a Career" seemed fine to his parents. The picture on the front showed just the kind of young man that his mother was sure he was going to grow up to be. Poised, well-groomed, well-tailored, clean, white-shirted and confident. His father was impressed by the pension plan, the health insurance plan and the probability of steady raises in pay. It was safe; it was respectable; unless he misbehaved himself in a spectacular way he could depend upon an uninterrupted work life of forty years. It was ideal. Into the bank went Chester.

He did his work adequately. In fact, it made few demands upon him. He was easily able to carry out the routine procedures for which it called. He was not bored or unhappy. He was just not really interested, either in the day-to-day work of the present or in the possibilities of different or more advanced work in the future. The working hours passed, closing time came, and that was another day.

So the years went by. They brought minor promotions. On the strength of one of them, Chester got married. Perhaps it would be more strictly true to say that Ingrid married him. She was two years older than he was, a strong, healthy, fresh-faced Swedish girl, the daughter of one of his father's friends who worked for the same contractor. Perhaps Chester's rather apathetic character called to some latent motherliness in her; or perhaps he found it pleasant to relax behind her protective vitality; however it was, they got along well together and the marriage prospered. They decided not to have children for the first year or two, and Ingrid continued to work as a waitress in a restaurant near to the bank.

They had begun to buy a home of their own and it was during some work on it that the accident happened. It was not a new house but in sound condition. Both fathers-in-law were practical men and, with their help and encouragement, the young couple undertook to remodel the kitchen. A few weekends were enough to complete the work. New cupboards of modern design replaced their old-fashioned predecessors and new appliances gleamed whitely on all sides. Only the repainting remained to be done. With four to lend a hand, this work went quickly. To reach his part of the ceiling, Chester stood on a chair placed on a side cupboard. A chance bump from one of the others and the damage was done. Chester fell heavily.

The next few days were a pleasant revelation to him. Ingrid gave him his breakfast in bed before leaving for work. With the newspaper and the radio, the morning passed quickly. She came home during her lunch hour and, after she had gone again, Chester settled happily down for an afternoon's television and sandwiches. Ingrid was solicitude itself in the evening. For Chester, the day was an unqualified success. During those which followed, he unconsciously learned a fatal lesson. He had found an easy way to avoid responsibility.

When he could no longer delay his return to the bank, he went back to work, but with many expressions of misgiving. Later, when an unpleasant rush of work was imminent, it would seem to him, when he woke in the morning, that his back was paining him. He would remain in bed that day, and Ingrid would undertake to make the necessary explanations, as she passed on her way to work in her restaurant. Gradually, Chester began to take advantage of this excuse more and more often. It was not that his back did not hurt him. Sometimes it did. But it did not incapacitate him, and with an effort of the will, he could have carried out his work. But instead, a kind of instinctive connection became established within him, between the thought, "This is something I do not want to do," and the thought, "My back is hurting again." It got him out of canvassing for the Community Chest; it saved him many hours of toiling in the yard; it ensured that Ingrid stoked the furnace and put up the storm windows in the fall; it excused any passing-over for promotion at the bank; it gave him a claim on the sympathy and help of anyone he met. If he was feeling ill-tempered, which happened with increasing frequency, it provided him with an irrefutable excuse.

Ingrid continued to go out to work. Her pleasant manner and ability presently advanced her to the post of supervisor. Her wages became a more and more important factor in the family budget, and she found more and more satisfaction in her work at the restaurant. It became unthinkable that she should give it up. The question of children was imperceptibly shelved. She cared for Chester with a warmhearted maternal care. As far as she could, she protected him from the hard world outside. She undertook the tasks that "poor Chester" would have discharged if only his back would have allowed him. Loving, careful, kindly, and motherly, she was probably the worst kind of wife he could have married. She helped to enwrap the toils of *accidie* around him until there was no escape. As a result, he lived out his life deprived of all joy, challenge, and achievement, a victim of this insidious, willful, gloomy, complaining, lazy sin.

Accidie takes many forms. The contemporary movements of disillusionment and cynicism are further examples. Neither the middle-aged and socially respectable half-invalid, nor the shook-up adolescent would relish the suggestion that they are the same kind of people. But, in fact, they are both caught in the snare of *accidie*. The teenage groups, which are a noisome product of the mid-twentieth century, bear all the characteristic marks of this sin. Their random and apparently meaningless acts of violence are an expression of nihilism and lack of personal motivation. The roots of this are not merely economic. It is not only the bitter and deprived youngsters from the big-city slums who are infected with this antisocial disease, but also adolescents from the split-level homes of the new suburbs. The roots are deeper than economic. They are spiritual. In these gangs we see yet another working out into action of that same sullen, brooding, sour indolence which is the very essence of *accidie*.

A more intellectual manifestation of the same underlying sickness is the so-called "beat generation." Their outward characteristics are drearily typical: the straggly beard, the sloppy trousers, the dirty shirt, the sagging sweater, the general air of lack of washing and combing. The tendency to drug addiction is a significant symptom.

Noel Coward gave expression to the feelings of his own lost postwar generation in England in the 1920s. His words could be equally well spoken for the beatnik of today.

> In this strange confusion
> Chaos and illusion,
>> People seem to lose their way.
> Nothing left to strive for
> Love, or keep alive for.

"Cavalcade"

Accidie is a failure of spiritual nerve. It greets all splendid things with a weary or a worldly-wise snigger. The bottom has fallen out of life. Vanity of vanities, all is vanity.

> This is the way the world ends
> Not with a bang but a whimper.
>> T. S. Eliot: "The Hollow Men"

Those who remember the years of the Great Depression know that one of the great evils of unemployment is that it weakens the moral fiber of a man in this very same way. It degrades him by laying him open to the sin of *accidie,* with all the evil results which can come so easily from it. Those labor leaders who are advocating a four-day week would be well advised to consider exactly what it is they are doing. Honest hard work honestly done is not something to be avoided. There are many worse things that can happen to a man than to be obliged to put in a full week's work. Those who escape from work may find themselves delivered into something much less enjoyable. The same is, of course, equally true of the wealthy man who, as the phrase is, "has no need to work." The phrase is a false one. Everyone has need to work at something worthwhile. The negation of this truth leads straight to *accidie.*

Another example of this sin is to be seen in attempts to contract out of the world and to escape into some bomb shelter or ivory tower. This is an ever-present temptation to artists in whatever medium. Not all are robust enough to resist it. Examples come readily to mind of painters, musicians, writers, sculptors, and others who have withdrawn from the offensive real world of men into an esoteric one of their own. In the realm of modern philosophy, we find their counterpart in the work of Sartre and the existentialists. In politics, what the French call *"Je m'en futisme"* is a manifestation of the same attitude. Everything's a racket. I couldn't care less. You look after yourself. I'm all right, Jack.

What passes for "tolerance" is sometimes *accidie* under another name. There is a true tolerance, of course, which represents the right of honest men to differ honestly. This is a rightly cherished freedom of democracy. But this good word "tolerance" is sometimes extended to cover something less respectable. This is the false tolerance that is merely an acceptance of evil and an acquiescence in it. To take a stand may be hard and unpopular. It may bring ridicule and contempt. Perhaps there are powerful interests on the other side. Tolerance is a sacred cow in our Western democracy. So, to avoid being branded as intolerant, a man may not take the necessary stand and may allow the error to go unchallenged. This is not tolerance. It is cowardice, moral sloth, *accidie*.

In the parable of the talents, Jesus classified as a "wicked servant" the one who did nothing. He was not a thief, nor a murderer, nor a drunkard, nor an adulterer. He simply hid his talent in the ground. By this parable, the wicked person is one who has something he can use for God but fails to make use of it. It is this same negative sin of *accidie,* the sin of doing nothing with the gifts with which we have been entrusted.

We have seen how complex and subtle this sin is and how varied are the forms in which it finds expression. Three main elements go to make it up. They can be distinguished from each other, though in practice they almost always tend to meet and mingle: gloom, sloth, irritation. The temptation to *accidie* is one which very quickly gains in strength when once a man has begun to yield ground to it. It does more than many other sins that may look uglier to make life fruitless and unhappy.

It attacks every part of our nature. There is bodily sloth. Lazy people are always with us. They are the people who manage to leave the hard work for others; they are the first to be missing when a job needs to be done; their mark is the charming smile and the ready excuse. We all know them. There is probably some of that kind of ingredient in the makeup of all of us.

Then there is intellectual sloth. This type is not quite so obvious but he is still extremely common. He takes his opinions from whatever source happens along, whether it be the latest newspaper columnist, superficial magazine article, or slick radio commentator. He never questions, checks, or even weighs what he receives because that would involve mental exertion. Very many people talk loudly about politics and even more loudly about religion, and yet often the people who talk loudest have the least right to an opinion. They have merely appropriated what someone else has suggested to them. The mentally slothful man takes the ready-made opinions of others in order to avoid the effort of arriving at his own. His opinions are not really opinions at all but a chance collection of prejudices. Prejudice is a great labor-saving device: it enables a man to advance opinions without taking the trouble to get the facts.

Moral sloth is another kind. It expresses itself in putting off unpleasant duties and decisions. This interview will be difficult, so let's find an excuse for postponing it. This decision will be a hard and unwelcome one. Let's find a reason for not taking it.

The last kind of sloth is spiritual. It is quite possible to be very active externally and at the same time extremely slothful in spirit. As physical sloth undermines the body, and as mental sloth debilitates the mind, so spiritual sloth weakens the soul. The man who neglects his prayers, his Communions, his Bible study, is not going to grow spiritually strong. As with other forms of sloth, he is going to have to pay the price of his laziness. The price will be the drying up of the wells from which his soul should be drawing its refreshment and without which it will grow parched and dry.

The way in which the Israelites reacted to Moses' leadership is an excellent example from the Old Testament of this same cowardly and lazy sin. They had been enslaved by the Egyptians; they were living degraded lives, whipped to work by their oppressors. Along came Moses to rescue them. He spoke encouragingly of the happiness awaiting them in the Promised Land. Their children could grow up as free men there, and they themselves would once more be a nation, fulfilling their destiny under the will of God. It was a glorious prospect; but it called for decisive action; it required a readiness to venture, to take a chance. Their reply was the classic one of *accidie*. "Let us alone," they said, "that we may serve the Egyptians." Eventually, Moses managed to put enough heart into them that they followed him into the desert, grumbling and "murmuring," as the Bible puts it, at every stage of the journey. When the time came for them to cross the Jordan river and to fight for their inheritance in the new land, although in the end they found somewhere the courage to follow where Joshua led, the first reports of what waited them were sufficient to threaten a complete undoing of all that the toughening process of their years in the desert had been intended to do for them. They raised the same old cowardly, lazy cry.

And all the children of Israel murmured against Moses and against Aaron: and the whole congregation said unto them, would God that we had died in the land of Egypt! or would God we had died in this wilderness! And wherefore hath the Lord brought us unto this land, to fall by the sword, that our wives and our children should be a prey? Were it not better for us to return into Egypt?

Numbers 14:2-3

Accidie is the enemy of all achievement; it is failure of nerve, the deadening drag of spiritual inertia. The contrary virtue to it is diligence. This is what is needed in the long pull of a man's whole seventy or eighty years on earth. It is the ability to endure manfully in small things. Life is a long-distance race, not a hundred-yard dash. It is the distance, not the pace, that tries us. "He that shall endure to the end, the same shall be saved."

I once came across a moving verse written by a mother whose young son had gone off blithely and gallantly to war and had found death waiting for him there.

> Courage and Fortitude are lovely words,
> And lovely are the virtues they define.

Yours was the Courage, laughing soldier,
May the Fortitude be mine.

Diligence—fortitude—perseverance; these are the qualities of character that project the soul from *accidie*. The determination to keep on keeping-on, not to grow weary in well-doing.

G. K. Chesterton once pointed out that if you leave a thing alone, you leave it to a torrent of change. If you leave a white post alone, it will soon be a black post. If you particularly want it to be white, you must always be painting it again. Like the Red Queen, we have to run if we want to stay even in the same place, let alone make any progress.

One of the strongest defenses against *accidie* is a personal "rule of life." Some people don't take too kindly to this idea. It seems to them to be reducing religion to a matter of a cold observance of a few rules. But this is not what is meant by a rule of life. The purpose of such a private rule is to ensure that certain things that ought to get priority do in fact get the priority that they should receive. A rule of so many minutes a day for our prayers means that our prayers do not get crowded out. Most of us have set and regular times for our daily meals. A rule about frequency of Communion ensures that the soul is fed as well as the body. A few simple rules such as these can form the basis for a healthy spiritual life. Each of us can draw up his own. Every churchman of course should have a private rule about what proportion of his income he will return each week to God. If we decide on what our priorities are to be and make a simple private rule about them, the secondary things will fall into place around them.

Another defense against *accidie* is to turn promptly and strenuously to work. Due provision must be made for recreation if a healthy balance is to be maintained; but mere idleness, just doing nothing, is to be avoided at all times. "Killing time" is a barbarous phrase for a barbarous thing. It is a waste of the life which God gave for a better purpose. We have seen that it is also very dangerous spiritually. Our Lord warned us about the man whose soul was swept and garnished, but who had neglected to take God in as the new tenant. The house was empty. So the evil spirit—the evil habit—which had been expelled, returned, and seven others worse still; and the last state of the man was worse than the first. The negative emptiness that is the result of *accidie* leaves the house of the soul open to any evil suggestion or prompting that may come along. The old proverb is no less true for being old: "Satan finds some mischief still for idle hands to do."

The more we remember and understand the real sufferings of other people, of those who have to face the real privations and trials of life, the less we shall give way to this idle, causeless, self-pitying gloom of *accidie*. "I felt sorry for myself because I had no shoes," said the traveler, "until I met a man who had no feet." The Christian soul will look back, also and always, with thankful remembrance to Calvary where the love of God was poured out beyond measure for our redemption; will recall the love which God bears still and always for us; will look forward wtih grateful confidence to the glories of the life to come. The soul that dwells often upon these things has found an inner defense against *accidie*.

"Blessed are they that mourn," said Jesus, "for they shall be comforted." Depression of spirits is a very common feature of *accidie* but this is not the kind of "mourning" to which our Lord was referring. In times of grief, some people give way to an introspective and selfish type of mourning which, far from leading to "comfort," brings them down only deeper and deeper into a gloomy listlessness of mind and spirit. This is the kind of self-dramatizing grief that causes someone, for example, to preserve unchanged in every minute detail the room of some dear departed relation. Nothing must be touched or altered. The needs of the living must be held to be less important than this fetish of the dead. Perhaps the present family could put the dead man's room to good use, or perhaps use some of the furniture. But no, year after year, his widow insists that the melancholy ritual be observed, the pictures unchanged on the bookcase, the chair placed just so by the window. Such wrong use of sorrow is not what our Lord meant by mourning. It is no more than an escape from the present, a withdrawal from life into a dream world of self-pitying gloom.

Those are blessed who can use their sorrow as a means of drawing closer to Christ. This life is a vale of soul-making. The experiences that come to us as we pass through it are the means by which our character is formed. The soul can use everything that happens to it as raw material upon which to feed. Happy experiences can be used to increase our gratitude to God; times of reverence and awe can increase our sense of his majesty and of our own smallness in comparison; other people's troubles, by calling forth our pity and sympathy, can teach us something of the pity and sympathy that God feels for us. Our character is formed by the way we react to the experiences of life. Life is a grindstone; whether it wears a man down or polishes him up depends upon what he brings to it. There are no experiences that cannot be used by the soul for its advantage. Things that happen have reality in time and space; but our reaction to things that happen has reality in eternity.

The experience of pain and sorrow is no exception to this. God wastes nothing, not even these. A deep sorrow can teach a person courage, patience, endurance, gratitude to those who help him, and sympathy for those in similar grief. I have known it to bring a man back to God from a life of carelessness and pride. God can turn even such an experience to be the means of blessing and deepening of character. Many people can say with the Psalmist: "It is good for me that I have been in trouble, that I may learn thy statutes" (Psalm 119).

The thirteenth-century German abbess, Mechtchild of Magdeburg, once pictured a man at the gates of heaven. When he reached that point, he had to leave behind him all his riches and his earthly honors. He could take in with him only his character that he had formed on earth. He was a man who had suffered much during his lifetime, but now at last the time had come to say goodbye to sorrow forevermore. Before leaving the man whose companion she had been for many years, Pain spoke to our Lord, who stood at the gate of heaven, and she said: "Lord, I make many holy, though I myself am not holy; and I bring many to the gates of heaven, though I may never enter in myself."

But, for the Christian, sorrow is something more even than

a means of growth and deepening of character. It provides him with a way in which he can be united with Christ, who himself was a man of sorrows and acquainted with grief. Our Lord's life led him along a way of sorrow, and, when we tread a way of sorrow ourselves, we are walking along a road that is well known to him.

St. Paul, who knew more about pain than most people, once wrote: "I count all things but loss for the excellency of the knowledge of Christ Jesus my Lord . . . that I may win Christ and be found in him . . . . that I may know him and the power of his resurrection *and the fellowship of his sufferings*" (Philippians 3:8-9, 10). St. Paul found that his sufferings provided a way in which he could be united with Christ.

In the second century, there was a Bishop of Smyrna in Asia named Polycarp. When he was an old man, he was arrested in the course of a local persecution of Christians. When he was asked to recant, he replied: "I have served Christ for eighty-six years and I am not going to deny him now." He was burned alive. After his death, some friends wrote an account of his martyrdom and in this account his last prayer is recorded. "I give thee thanks, O God, that thou hast counted me worthy of this day and of this hour, that I should have a part in the cup of thy Christ." For the Christian, to suffer is to have a part with Christ. Pain and sorrow can be the means whereby a soul may be drawn into a closer fellowship with Christ than can be achieved in any other way.

More than this, pain provides the soul with one thing of its own that it may offer to God. Everything else we have has come from him. Our health, our food, our intelligence, our very life itself are his gifts. In the well-known words of the General Thanksgiving, our creation, preservation, and all the blessings of this life come from him and, beyond all these things, he has given us redemption by our Lord Jesus Christ, the means of grace and the hope of glory. What can we offer to him, that he has not already first given us? Pain is the only thing we have that God did not himself send us. Here is the one thing of our own that we can offer him.

> Lord, thou hast suffered more for me
> Than all the hosts of land and sea.
> So I would offer back to thee
> This token of my love.

This offering of pain, willingly endured for Christ's sake, is something that God can take and use. Every pain or sorrow that comes to us, if we accept it and offer it in union with Christ, can be taken up into his work of overcoming evil with good.

One day before the outbreak of the last war, I was speaking with a missionary who had recently returned from Japan. Together with his wife, he had spent several years in that country, first learning the language and then working in the school and hospital, teaching and healing such as he could reach. As relations between Japan and the Western nations worsened, his work became increasingly difficult and there were several ugly incidents. At last, some drunken Japanese soldiers broke into the mission compound one evening and, before the eyes of this man and his wife, bayoneted their seven-year-old daughter and threw her body into the mission cesspool. As we sat together one summer evening, back home in Canada, a few months after it had happened, her father told me about it. He added: "It was not a fitting death for so flower-like a little girl. But we have prayed that God may use it for his work of the redemption of the Japanese people."

For the Christian, to suffer is to share in the cross of Christ. Bitterness and rebellion under suffering separate the soul from God, for this was not Christ's way of meeting it. Suffering willingly endured and offered up to God, unites the soul with Christ and rapidly develops spiritual depth and power.

> Measure thy life by loss instead of gain,
> Not by the wine drunk, but by the wine poured forth,
> For love's strength standeth in love's sacrifice,
> And he who suffers most, has most to give.

The comfort that our Lord promised to those who mourn can be looked for in another way also. In life, we often notice that opposites result from the same causes and conditions. Courage and cowardice both arise from the same situations. The conditions are identical, but they are differently met. A situation that makes a coward of one man may call forth heroism in another. It is not possible to be brave except in circumstances likely to produce cowardice. In the same way, temptations that result in sin (when they are yielded to) are the cause of holiness (when they are resisted).

Within the Christian, struggling for holiness in this world, there must continually be present a hatred of sin and a sorrow for the part it has in him. The Church has always noticed that the holier a man may be becoming, the deeper is his sorrow for sin. In the same soul, at the same time, there is a deepening joy (as communion with God becomes more conscious and more constant) and a deepening sorrow (as the full horror of sin is more truly realized). So, for souls in pilgrimage through his earthly life, consummate joy is not possible without a corresponding and equal sorrow. But this is a mourning that is blessed indeed, and those who mourn in this way shall find an eternal comforting.

Perfect comfort and happiness are not possible on earth. At the bottom of even our deepest joy, there lurks always the remembrance of pain and death, of sin and parting. This is because we have no abiding city here. We are exiles looking for our true native land; and we frequently notice that even those people who have forgotten where this is, carry about with them a vague and inarticulate uneasiness, a kind of wistful longing for something they are not able to define.

By the waters of Babylon, we sat down and wept: when we remembered thee, O Sion.

As for our harps, we hanged them up: upon the trees that are therein.

For they that led us away captive required of us then a song, and melody in our heaviness: Sing us one of the songs of Sion.

How shall we sing the Lord's song: in a strange land?

Psalm 137:1-4

We do not belong here. We look for "a city which hath foundations, whose builder and maker is God," and we shall always have to carry about with us a burden of heaviness in our hearts during the time of our exile, until the coming of the "Great Day." Then, in the words of the Psalmist, our mouth shall be filled with laughter because they that have sown in tears shall reap at last in joy.

PRAYERS

Defend us, O Lord, against idleness and the misuse of time which can never come back; lest our lives he unprofitable to thee, mischievous to others, and without honor or joy to ourselves; through Jesus Christ our Lord. Amen.

O God of everlasting strength and infinite compassion, who knowest our weakness in drawing after temptation and back from pain: we pray thee, not that we shall never sin, but that we may leave no sin unrepented; not that we shall never suffer, but that we may learn in all things the patience of Christ crucified; not that we shall never fail, but that our souls may go to thee in failure and in success; not that our road be always plain and unperilous, but that we may persevere unto the end, through Jesus Christ our Lord. Amen.

> Fight the good fight with all thy might,
> Christ is thy strength and Christ thy right;
> Lay hold on life, and it shall be
> Thy joy and crown eternally.
>
> Run the straight race through God's good grace,
> Lift up thine eyes, and seek his face;
> Life with its way before us lies,
> Christ is the path, and Christ the prize.

SCRIPTURE

I know thy works, that thou art neither cold nor hot: I would thou wert cold or hot. So then, because thou art lukewarm, and neither cold nor hot, I will spue thee out of my mouth.

Revelation 3:15-16

He that endureth to the end shall be saved.

Matthew 10:22

SPIRIT AND MATTER

Beauty is one means of anticipating the achievement which all of us hope for at the further end of eternity—the complete subjugation of matter to the uses and ends of the spirit. Here in what is beautiful, we see that attainment before our eyes and its presence sustains us in the long journey.

Professor Hocking: Valedictory lecture at Yale.

Chapter 7

COVETOUSNESS

Avarice, after the description of Saint Augustine, is a desire in heart to have earthly things . . . And the difference between Avarice and Covetousness is this: Covetousness is for to covet such things as thou hast not; and Avarice is to withhold and keep such things as thou hast, without rightful need.

Chaucer, *Canterbury Tales*

The Contrary Virtue to Covetousness is Liberality

Blessed are the poor in spirit

COVETOUSNESS is an inordinate love of worldly goods. The good things of this world are given to us by God for our comfort and enjoyment as we travel along our journey to the world which is to come. There is certainly nothing wrong about them in themselves, although puritans of all kinds have often argued that there is. Christians are perfectly right to enjoy riches with a grateful heart, as they come their way. But they are by their very nature transitory, and pass away with the passing world. The trouble is that people are always liable to start desiring them too much. Because of this, men deliver themselves into much pain and sorrow which they could otherwise have avoided.

The covetous man has his values reversed. He sins against both God and himself. He offends God who is alone the giver of all good and who alone is to be desired above everything else. He also brings much unhappiness upon himself. St. Paul warned his young friend Timothy of the bitterness of heart that is the dark fruit of this sin.

The love of money is the root of all kinds of evil; which while some have coveted after, they have erred from the faith and pierced themselves through with many sorrows.

The goods of this world are of three kinds: those which are necessary, those which are useful, and those which are luxuries. The first two categories are much smaller than most people suppose.

The bare necessities of life are not many. If a person has wholesome food, adequate clothing, and shelter, he has all that he needs for a long and happy life. The food need not be delicate, nor the clothing of the latest fashion, nor the shelter in the choicest part of town. Human necessities, properly considered, are really much simpler than is commonly supposed. A visit to a monastery can quickly demonstrate this fact. There men are to be found who are living perfectly satisfactory and healthy lives on less cash outlay for a week than many of us would spend on a single dinner.

In addition to necessities, certain goods are useful. The bodies of most of us welcome a reasonable degree of comfort. A man requires the tools of his trade, whatever that may be. The fruit of men's thought down the ages and the varied inheritance of art in all its forms make their contribution to the development of mind and soul. Books, pictures, and music make a full man. These are useful things, but they cost comparatively little. In many parts of the world, certainly in those countries where this book may expect to find readers, these things are available free, or at minimal cost, to everyone. When we come to examine them, we find that the really useful things, like the necessities, are fewer in number, and certainly cost less, than many people imagine.

The third kind of worldly goods are luxuries, and it is these that many men desire and can never have enough of. The history of nations moves in a well-established cycle that the world has seen repeated many times. A civilization is built up by discipline; it prospers and grows strong; its strength brings riches and luxury; then, sooner or later, the process of decay begins; the once hardy people become pleasure-loving and soft; the luxuries of one generation become the necessities of the next; eventually the civilization falls before another whose cycle is just beginning.

On a smaller scale, much the same history can sometimes be seen in families. The founder of the family is an honest, hard-working man who by determination and drive establishes his business. His son has been brought up against the harsh background of economic reality and knows exactly how many cents make a dollar. But the grandson has never known poverty, either at first or second hand. For him, luxury has become a necessity. His expensive tastes and soft character all too often bring to ruin the achievements of those before him. "From clogs to clogs in three generations," runs the Yorkshire proverb.

The covetous man is the man whose desire for luxuries can never be satisfied. He struggles to acquire certain possessions that had previously been beyond his reach and he is pleased with them for a while. Then those luxuries lose their novelty and begin to seem like necessities. So he starts to feel discontented. His covetousness makes him unhappy until he can own a further series of luxuries which in their turn lose their power to give him pleasure because by now he has his desire fixed on acquiring something else. So the unhappy man goes round upon the tread-wheel of his covetousness, always driven, always revolving, and never arriving at stillness and contentment.

> Here we go round the prickly pear
> Prickly pear, prickly pear
> Here we go round the prickly pear
> At five o'clock in the morning.

This paraphrase of an old children's game, which occurs in T.S. Eliot's poem, "The Hollow Men," well expresses this endless round of unsatiable covetousness. Many people are caught by it, in our acquisitive Western civilization. The pear can't be eaten and yet their hunger for it can never be satisfied. Round and round they go, not only at five o'clock in the morning but all through the day and far into the night. Money and investments, business opportunities, houses and lands, stocks and dividends; these keep many people in a ceaseless revolving but, like the prickly pear, turn out to be strangely and deceptively unsatisfying in the last resort. "It is but lost labour [wrote the Psalmist] that ye haste to rise up early and so late take rest, and eat the bread of sorrow. Except the Lord build the house, their labour is but lost that build it." As St. Paul says: the covetous man "pierces himself through with many sorrows." Those who like everything they have are happier than those who try to have everything they like.

In practice, it is difficult to distinguish between the useful and the luxurious. But, in our moral life, whenever it is difficult to draw the line, it is usually all the more important that the line should be drawn. Each of us should be taking constant care that our possessions are not getting a grip upon us. It is good to have money and the things that money can buy. But it is good also to make sure once in a while that we haven't lost the things that money can't buy.

The good things of life fall into two well-defined classes: those things that are of such nature that if one person enjoys them another cannot, and those things that, if I enjoy them, you and others can enjoy them too. Covetousness involves desire for exclusive possession. Along with lust and anger, it is an assertion of the "self" against the "community." The root of it is the desire for possession (not sharing) and for hoarding (not use). The Christian will be wise to be content with the necessities of a simple life: food, clothing, shelter—and to seek his real goods in knowledge, beauty, friendship, service, religion —things which increase by being shared. The wise man is not the man who has learned to desire nothing, but the man who has learned to desire the right things.

The anonymous author of the *Theologia Germanica,* a mystic of the fourteenth century, maintained that the very cause of the "Fall" lay in this fatal drive for exclusive possession.

It is said, it was because Adam ate the apple that he was lost and fell. I say it was because of his claiming something for his own, and because of his I, Mine, Me and the like. Had he eaten seven apples, and yet never claimed anything for his own, he would not have fallen.

Dostoevski's "parable of the onion" in *The Brothers Karamazov* is one of the most telling, outside of the New Testament, of the destructive effects of this selfish sin. The motherly Grushenka relates it in Book III of the third part of that remarkable novel.

Once upon a time, there was a peasant woman, and a very wicked woman she was. She died and did not leave a single good deed behind her. The devils caught her and plunged her into the lake of fire. So her guardian angel stood and wondered what good deed of hers he could remember to tell to God. "She once pulled up an onion in her garden," he said, "and gave it to a beggar woman." And God answered, "You take that onion then, hold it out to her in the lake, and let her take hold and be pulled out. If you can pull her out of the lake, let her come to Paradise, but if the onion breaks, then the woman must stay where she is." The angel ran to the woman and held out the onion to her. "Come," said he, "catch hold and I'll pull you out." And he began cautiously pulling her out. He had just pulled her right out, when the other sinners in the lake, seeing how she was being drawn out, began catching hold of her so as to be pulled out with her. But she began kicking them. "I'm to be pulled out, not you. It's my onion, not yours." As soon as she said that, the onion broke, and the woman fell back into the lake. The angel wept and went away.

Man's appetite is infinite, and "enough" has been well defined as "a little more than you have." So long as our hearts are covetously set on material things, our happiness will depend less upon what we have than upon what we see other people have and we don't have. The poorest man in a city slum today has many comforts and conveniences that Aristotle and Erasmus never conceived. Yet they lived full, rich, and happy lives never feeling the lack of material things of which they had no knowledge, whereas a poor man today is miserable because he lacks what others enjoy. He is not to be blamed for being miserable. Society is at fault if it allows some of its members (unless they deserve it) to fall far below the generally accepted standards of comfort of their day. But such things are relative. Many things that are regarded as necessities today are not in fact really necessary to man as a human being. As men in earlier ages have proved, a full and successful human life can be lived without them.

A small country community, well known to me, provides a modern illustration. A few years ago, it was quite cut off from the main industrial life of the country. The people lived by fishing, logging, and catering to summer tourists. They were healthy, devout, prolific, and long-lived. Recreation consisted chiefly of dances held in the community hall on Saturday nights and simple whist drives on other occasions. Some people might call it a "backward" community, but this is a question-begging description. It depends on what you mean by backward. Before you can decide that, you must first decide the direction in which you think it is desirable to go.

Into this "backward" community there moved a large mining company, and a mine was opened up. The pattern is familiar enough and there is no need to recount in detail all that resulted. The largest single factor was that much more money became available. A few families acquired various urbanized appliances that had been unknown in the district before. Immediately, everyone else had to have them or feel deprived and discontented.

So, fairly soon, nearly everyone else bought them too. What is usually referred to as the "standard of living" rose all round. But, so far as can be seen, the people are no healthier or happier than they were. They possess more things. The horizon of their desires has extended. This has been confidently described as "progress." I am not so sure.

No sentimental and impossible return to the old simpler days is being advocated here. Developments such as this are inevitable and take place in the lives of nations and individuals. Whether they involve "progress" or not depends upon what is done with the new wealth. For some it may mean a deepening of education, knowledge, and culture, an ability to live a fuller and richer life as a human being. If so, this is progress indeed. But, for others, there is likely to be an increase in the covetous drive to possess more things, and to use the new wealth in self-indulgent and harmful ways. Material advance is not necessarily progress. A man's life consisteth not in the abundance of the things which he possesseth. A man's possessions are morally neutral, neither good nor bad in themselves. What matters is his attitude toward them.

Art Watson's father had been a shiftless and irresponsible character, a cheerful, easygoing kind of fellow who drifted in a totally unconcerned manner from one job to another, not bothering his head about such things as how bills got to be paid, or how a wife and children got to be fed and clothed. One of his favorite sayings when things were going badly was that he would live till he died. Eventually he did die, when Art was in Grade X. He left little money and no insurance; no one had expected that he would. There were five other children, all younger than Art, and some money had to be earned as soon as possible. The local hardware store had a vacancy for a young clerk and, the day after the funeral, Art reported there for duty. As the years passed, the other children took their share in earning the family income. By the time Art was twenty, the worst was over. He had gained valuable experience, he had learned the hardware business pretty thoroughly, and he was ready to strike out on his own. With backing from a few of the more well-to-do men in the town, most of whom knew him and sized him up as a good risk, Art opened a small store of his own in a new shopping center which was just being completed. It was hard work, but it prospered from the start. By doing all his own bookwork and keeping all overhead down to a minimum, Art was able to pay the interest on his loans and to retire the capital steadily. In ten years, the store was his own. He was now thirty and, for some years, had been earning considerably more than he spent, even allowing for the loan repayments. His mother frequently urged him "to get some fun out of life like your dear father did." But Art remembered his dear father only too well. He had a contempt for the lazy and the irresponsible. He knew other men like that too, young men of his own age. None of them could have achieved what he had, starting as he had done with less than nothing. He preferred to save his money. His holdings increased steadily and he derived great satisfaction from them. At the end of five more years, he acquired the grocery business in the building next to him and managed both the stores himself with the help of a bookkeeper and an extra salesclerk. He was now thirty-five. It was time for a wife.

He knew little of women. Once or twice on business trips he had bought and paid for a few sex experiences, having ascertained the going rate beforehand; but he had had next to no social contact with the young women of the town where he had lived. He was conscious of being rather dull company. They preferred the easy spender and the young man with plenty of evenings free to squire them around. Well let them, thought Art, and comforted himself with the sardonic reflections that the car they rode in was not paid for nor the young man's bank balance approaching the size of his own. But, if he was going to marry, it was time to do so, and a well-established businessman like himself should have a wife. Besides, his mother would not last much longer. He would need someone to look after him and cook his meals. A housekeeper would be very expensive. She would cost almost as much as another salesclerk. No, what he needed was a wife, and one with money of her own, if possible. He looked around carefully, found a young woman who seemed to fill the bill, and managed to clinch the agreement. Her parents were impressed with the statement of his financial position that he gave them. Millicent was no raving beauty and a better offer seemed unlikely.

So Art entered upon the married state. His mother died soon afterward as he had calculated. Indeed, it turned out to be for less than a year that he had to provide for two women in his house. It all worked out very satisfactorily. His wife took over where his mother had left off.

Instead of being an oldish young man, Art now imperceptibly became a youngish old man. He was settled, his household arrangements were taken care of, above all he was growing richer every year. Of the rest of his life there is little more to tell. Because of his wealth, people courted him. But, when it came right down to cases, few could get much out of him. The canvassers for the Community Chest soon learned not to expect too much. He had worked hard for his money while others played (he was fond of saying), he paid taxes enough as it was, let the city take care of the needy, they were no concern of his. Poor Art, the rough experiences of his early life had robbed him of what it is to be a full man. The loving and the giving of the world had passed him by.

Few victims of this sin of covetousness recognize its full evil and danger; but all of us dislike it when we see it in others. The word "miser" has a contemptuous ring about it. The very word, by the way, comes from the Latin word meaning "wretched" or "unhappy." It suggests that the covetous man is in fact a fundamentally unhappy one. The sin produces a hard and grasping character. The covetous man is so obsessed with his desire to amass wealth for himself that there is no room in his heart for generosity. He is so consumed with the desire to "get" that he finds no happiness in giving. He is usually quite careless and indifferent about the state of those less well off than he. His sins cuts him off from really human and loving contacts with his fellows. He would rather have possessions than people.

When the seven deadly sins come in to greet Faustus in the play by Christopher Marlowe, the author introduces covetousness to the audience with these words:

I am Covetousness, begotten of an old churl, in an old leathern bag; and, might I have my wish, I would desire that this house and all the people in it were turned to gold, that I might lock you up in my good chest: O, my sweet gold.

This is the truth which lies behind the classic legend of King Midas. This ancient king, so the story runs, was given his choice of what gift he would have from the gods. Although immensely wealthy already, he wanted even greater wealth. So he asked that all he touched should be turned to gold. And it was so. He was delighted and enchanted. He touched a table in his palace and immediately it was changed to solid gold. He went out into his rose garden and spent some time touching the petals and transforming the common, everyday flowers into priceless golden masterpieces. Presently his daughter came out to look for him. She ran up and kissed him. Whereupon King Midas found that what he now had was no longer a living daughter of flesh and blood, but an exceedingly valuable statue of a young girl, in solid gold.

It was the danger of this sin that caused our Lord to require the rich young ruler to sell all that he had and give to the poor. The young man was very wealthy. He could not rise to the demand and turned sorrowfully away. As our Lord watched him go, he remarked sadly: "How hardly shall they that have riches enter into the Kingdom of God." Riches are not evil but they are dangerous. They draw a man away from reliance on God. Unless he is careful, they lead him into pride and covetousness. "If riches increase," says the Psalmist, "set not your heart upon them." A well-known reproof of the man who allows himself to be beguiled by his possessions occurs in the story of the rich fool, in St. Luke's Gospel. He had no room for all his goods, he made arrangements to pull down his present barns and build bigger ones that would be large enough to contain all that he had to store away; then he would take it easy for many years to come. He had it all planned. Then it turned out that he died that night. As the saying goes: "You can't take it with you." Every priest knows that there is no difference, when it comes to his deathbed, between a rich man and a poor one. Certainly at that dread hour, but often long before it, the covetous man finds that he has been deceived. Sin is a deceiver; it is death pretending to be life. The overwhelming desire for possessions is a snare and a delusion.

Because thou sayest, I am rich, and increased with goods, and have need of nothing; and knowest not that thou art wretched, and miserable, and poor, and blind and naked: I counsel thee to buy of me gold tried in the fire, that thou mayest be rich; and white raiment, that thou mayest be clothed, and that the shame of thy nakedness do not appear; and anoint thine eyes with eye-salve, that thou mayest see.

Revelation 3:17-18

The contrary virtue to covetousness is liberality. This is a royal road to happiness. We all know people who seem always to be doing things for others, sharing or giving away their own possessions, and who seem to find a great happiness and satisfaction in it. This is something that our Lord strongly recommended, ("It is more blessed to give than to receive"), but that the world finds very difficult to understand. To the covetous man it seems plain nonsense. But it is something that can be learned, and discovered to be true, if a person has determination and courage. Many a man, for example, who has taken the decision to tithe for his church, not because he wanted to but because he had come to feel that he ought to, has been surprised to find that a profound and satisfying happiness has been one of the by-products. Giving is something that no one else can do for us. We can't hire someone to do this on our behalf. The release it brings to the giver is found only through the actual experience of giving. It is an outgoing, loving attitude toward our fellow men. It is the very opposite of self-regarding and miserly covetousness, against which it is a tried and trusty weapon. It is a path to freedom and happiness.

> Half the happiness of living
> Comes from willing-hearted giving;
> Comes from sharing all our pleasures,
> From dividing all our treasures.

And the other half is loving
First the Lord, then all things living.
So each mortal should be sowing
Love seeds while his life is growing,
For all happiness in living
Comes from loving and from giving.

For the Christian, the motive for his giving is his grateful response to the infinite self-giving of God who gave himself for us. We love him because he first loved us.

"What! Giving again?" I ask in dismay,
"And must I keep giving and giving away?"
"Oh no," said the angel, piercing me through,
"Just keep giving till he stops giving to you."

If you are giving away to God, and to people in need, an amount that inconveniences you, an amount that obliges you to forego some luxury that you would otherwise have enjoyed, the noisome weed of covetousness is not likely to strike very deep roots in the soil of your heart. Liberality is a great defense against it.

"Blessed are the poor in spirit," said Jesus, "for theirs is the kingdom of heaven." This Beatitude is very commonly misunderstood. "Poor in spirit" does not mean "poor-spirited." The original Greek words in St. Matthew's Gospel cannot possibly be translated in that way. The meaning of "poor" underwent a development in the Bible. At first, it meant quite simply the economically poor. Later, in the Psalms and in the writings of the prophets, it came to have an ethical meaning also and so came to mean the lowly, those bowed down by misfortune. Later still, during the exile in Babylon, those Israelites who remained loyal to their religion were oppressed and persecuted. Those who were prepared to compromise were tolerated, as is always the case. So the godly and the oppressed came to mean the same thing. More and more, the word poor meant the godly poor, the suffering righteous, and they were to be the special care of the Messiah when he came. ("He shall deliver the needy when he crieth; the poor also and him that hath no helper." Ps. 72.)

Our Lord accepted this mission of the Messiah when he applied the prophecy from Isaiah to himself.

The Spirit of the Lord is upon me, because he hath anointed me to preach the gospel to the poor.

Luke 4:18

In the Beatitude, Jesus added the words "in spirit." This is a call to what the Church calls detachment from material possessions. Other religions also have advocated this, but not for the same reasons. The stoic says: "Blessed are the self-sufficient for they are kingly." Like our Lord, stoicism taught men to be independent of the things they possess, but the root of this was pride, determination to be one's own master. The Christian reason is so that God may be more fully the master. The Hindu says: "Blessed are the detached for the things of the world have no value." The Christian does not say this. The things of the world have value and are good, but they are relatively unimportant. This Beatitude asserts the blessedness, the happiness of those who are detached from worldly possessions. "Deliver me from the things that I cannot do without," wrote Thomas à Kempis. We must learn to sit lightly on our possessions. We must not let them become too important to us. If your house burned down with all that is in it, how much of a fundamental loss would that be to you? After some disaster like a hurricane, many people are faced with that kind of question. They are forced to discover the degree to which certain material things have established a hold over them. For some time during the war, I was the priest of a parish in England that suffered several air raids. One morning, after the German bombers had left and the fires were out, the families whose homes had been destroyed were standing in front of the ruins. All the old familiar things had gone: the dinner service that had belonged to the grandparents, the furniture that had been bought when they were first married, the favorite fishing rod, the photographs of the children. In many cases, nothing at all remained to them except the clothes that they were wearing when they had taken shelter six or seven hours before. Again and again, I was astounded to observe that, after the first shock was over, people seemed to experience a strange feeling of freedom and release. The bondage to *things* had been forcibly broken and life had suddenly been reduced to its essential simplicities.

The virtue of detachment consists in preserving that kind of freedom from material possessions, even while living an ordinary life in the midst of them. The person who has learned this lesson has taken a great step toward serenity and peace of mind. "Dost thou wish to possess the earth?" said St. Augustine. "Take heed lest thou be possessed by the earth." In Rudyard Kipling's wonderful novel *Kim,* the old Lama taught the young white boy many things as they journeyed together through the Indian countryside. Out of the deep wisdom of his many meditations, he spoke to Kim of this same virtue which Christians call detachment. Like all Buddhists, he was seeking for final release from the wheel of life and, although his goal was lower than that of the Christian, he understood the price that must be paid. He said, "Thou canst not choose freedom and go in bondage to the delight of life." This is the truth of which our Lord was speaking, when he said:

No man can serve two masters; for either he will hate the one, and love the other; or else he will hold to the one, and despise the other. Ye cannot serve God and mammon.

We must choose where our treasure is to be, because that is where our heart will be also. In order to be able to receive one kind of treasure, we have to be ready to let the other one go.

> How can you grasp God's offering?
> Your hands are full; they tightly cling
> To coarser stuff—how can you gain
> The new, and still the old retain?
> Let go the dross and grasp the gold,
> Both at one time you cannot hold.

The Christian is often compared to a soldier. In many of the sermons we hear on this topic, we are reminded of what may be called the positive aspects of the analogy: the soldier's courage, his obedience to the orders of his captain, his readiness to endure hardness, his ability to use and wear the weapons and

armor that God provides for him. It is true that the Christian
soldier needs these things. But there are also the negative dis-
ciplines of soldiering. No soldier goes on a campaign weighed
down with a mass of luggage. He is allowed to take only the
necessities. Nothing can be allowed to take priority over his
efficiency as a fighting man. He is a "detached" person. The
Christian is often compared to a pilgrim also. Here we have
another figure of a man who carries all he has in a single pack
on his shoulders. The man of whom this Beatitude speaks is the
man who has learned how to enjoy material possessions as they
come his way, but who, deep down within him, can remain detached from them ("poor in spirit"), so that they are not able
to fasten their grip upon him. This is Christian detachment. Such
souls as these have not laid up their treasures on the earth, and
so their heart has not been set there either. Our Lord tells us
that theirs is the kingdom of heaven. It follows; we get what
we choose.

PRAYERS

To teach thy wisdom, O Lord Christ: To lay up our treasures
not upon earth but in heaven: To set our hearts not on things
which pass away, but on things which abide for ever.

Grant us, O Lord, not to mind earthly things but to love things
heavenly; and even now, while we are placed among things that
are passing away, to cleave to those that shall abide.

O Almighty God, who alone canst order the unruly will and
affections of sinful men: Grant unto thy people that they may
love the thing which thou commandest and desire that which
thou doest promise: that so, among the sundry and manifold
changes of the world, our hearts may surely there be fixed
where true joys are to be found.

SCRIPTURE

Naked came I out of my mother's womb, and naked shall I
return thither. The Lord gave and the Lord hath taken away;
blessed be the name of the Lord.

Job I :21

As poor, yet making many rich; as having nothing, and yet possessing all things.

II Corinthians 8:9

Godliness with contentment is great gain. For we brought nothing into this world, and it is certain we can carry nothing out. And having food and raiment let us be therewith content. But they that will be rich fall into temptation and a snare, and into many foolish and hurtful lusts, which drown men in destruction and perdition. For the love of money is the root of all kinds of evil: which while some coveted after, they have erred from the faith, and pierced themselves through with many sorrows. But thou, O man of God, flee these things; and follow after righteousness, godliness, faith, love, patience, meekness.

Timothy 6:6-11

Let your conversation be without covetousness; and be content with such things as ye have: for he hath said, I will never leave thee, nor forsake thee.

Hebrews 13:5

FROM THE IMITATION OF CHRIST

Our advantage does not consist in winning or increasing possessions; it lies rather in being indifferent to such things, and eradicating the desire for them from our hearts. These harmful desires include not only love of riches, but also ambition for honours and vain praise. Remember that all these things pass away with the world. (Bk. III, chap. 27.)

Thomas à Kempis

Chapter 8

GLUTTONY

Gluttony is immeasurable appetite to eat or to drink . . . This sinne hath many spieces . . . The first is, for to eat before time. The second is, when a man getteth him too delicate meat or drink. The third is, when men take too much over measure. The fourth is a taste for rarities, with great intent to make and dress up his meat. The fifth is, for to eat greedily. These be the five fingers of the devil's hand, by which he draweth folk to this sinne.

Chaucer, *Canterbury Tales*

The Contrary Virtue to Gluttony is Temperance

Blessed are they that hunger and thirst after Righteousness

THE sin of gluttony is an inordinate desire for the pleasures connected with the sense of taste. Most people seem to think of it as consisting simply of overeating. This is certainly one of its forms, but it is a much more subtle sin than that. It arises from undue attention to the pleasures of the palate, whether by sheer excess in eating and drinking, or by the opposite fault of fastidiousness. It can take either a jovial or a refined form. The first form of it can lead a person into gross self-indulgence; the second into a persnickety overniceness and delicacy. So two kinds of people whom the world regards as quite opposite and unlike each other (and each of whom heartily despises the other) are in fact caught in the toils of this same sin. The flushed, loudmouthed, paunchy glutton and the quietly overrefined and self-indulgent glutton are brothers under the skin, however unwelcome the thought might be to each of them.

Like all sins, gluttony is the perversion of something that is good and right. Food and drink are necessities of bodily life. But, since they are necessities, they naturally offer a strong attraction. Sin enters in when a person responds excessively to this attraction.

Minor excesses in food and drink are dangerous because they tend to lead imperceptibly into habitual excess. Some women can never pass a box of candy without nibbling. A small excess like this may seem so small and unimportant as to be not worth even considering; but it is still an excess and therefore a step in the wrong direction. A habit of excess is built up from many such small acts continually repeated.

The grim problem of overdrinking has received considerable attention during these last few years, although much still remains to be done in educating the public about it. Again and again, those who have been defeated by it emphasize how their downward path began almost imperceptibly with small acts of excess scarcely worth bothering about at the time. The drink before the evening meal gradually became two, then three or four. The modest nightcap turned into two or three large slugs of whisky. Eventually, after a period of perhaps ten years or more, self-control had been quite lost and the unfortunate soul was tied and bound by the chain of alcoholism.

The results of overeating are less obvious than those of over-drinking and therefore many people who are habitually glutton-ous at the table escape the censure that falls upon the habitual drunkard. But, in our opulent society, obesity is in danger of becoming a national characteristic. This widespread and ex-tremely unattractive result of gluttony makes fortunes for the manufacturers of reducing foods. The situation could be more easily remedied if people quite simply did not overeat in the first place.

It has often been pointed out that our present ways of living have several disturbing similarities with those of Roman civiliza-tion as it passed into its degenerate period. One feature of Roman society in its later years was a social convenience known as the vomitorium. The guests at a banquet would gorge them-selves on rich food and wine to the point where their systems could take no more. Then they would leave the room for a few moments, induce the act of vomiting (usually by putting the fingers down the throat), and return refreshed to the dining room. Such a perversion of the true use of food and drink rightly seems disgusting to us. Our manners are more refined. There is however an uncomfortable similarity between this honest and forthright method of dealing with overindulgence and the reducing pills and slimming foods of our own day. In both cases, the treatment is made necessary because the body has become stuffed and gorged by a gluttonous indulgence in the pleasures of the table.

Gluttony has also its refined and overdelicate form. This is the sin of those people who must have their food exactly to suit their exacting taste. The coffee must be freshly ground, the egg cooked to the exact fraction of a minute, the steak grilled to the right extent, the sauce blended from the precise ingredients. A good deal of foolish posing often enters here. There are peo-ple whose palate is not really so delicately educated as they would have us think but who sometimes put on a great show of knowl-edge in these matters from a desire to impress. The fault of such people is not gluttony but vanity. But there are others, more sophisticated and more discriminating, to whom these culinary matters are of real and great importance. This is by no means to condemn the skillful chef and the man who can appreciate the result of his work. It is a question of degree. The person who can no longer enjoy a simple and wholesome meal because the lack of some refinement has spoiled it for him is caught in the snares of gluttony. He has forgotten what the purpose of eating is. Similarly, the man who devotes an undue amount of time, energy, and interest (which could be better spent) in searching out or concocting some new ways of delighting his palate has fallen into gluttony. We must eat to live, not live to eat. The gluttonous man has reversed the natural order of values.

Physical grossness is a frequent result of this sin. Less apparent but more serious are its effects on the soul. The gluttonous person allows his bodily instincts to control him and so becomes materialistic in outlook and desire. The man who is constantly thinking about food is unlikely to rise to great spiritual heights. The chief danger of spending much time in bars and cocktail lounges is not so much drunkenness (though that is of course a danger) as the general materialization and coarsening of outlook which results. The habitual barfly sinks to a low moral, spiritual, and mental level.

Gluttony exalts the flesh at the expense of the spirit, and so it is closely connected with the other fleshly sin of lust. The overpampered body is easily inflamed to casual sensuality. Anyone finding it difficult to preserve chastity should certainly avoid rich food and drink. As St. Gregory bluntly says:

It is plain to all that lust springs from gluttony, when in the very distribution of the bodily members, the genitals appear placed beneath the belly. And hence, when the one is inordinately pampered, the other is doubtless excited to wantonness.

Moralia in Job

The professional seducer has always well understood that sweet foods and alcohol help to soften resistance. Men who like to entice their women friends into casual fornication, know the value of this kind of preparation in the early stages. There has been many an act of lust committed, after the way has been prepared by gluttony and intemperance, which would never have been committed otherwise. A respectable family man I knew, a good husband and father, became drunk before he realized what he was doing at a party one evening. While he was still drunken, he committed an act of grave sexual indecency, was arrested by the police, and subsequently convicted with all the usual horrible attendant publicity. In his right senses, he would have been incapable of such conduct. But gluttony, in the form of overindulgence in alcohol, had undermined the habitual moral defenses of his character and a shameful act resulted, quite out of keeping with his normal way of life. Gluttony had opened for lust a door which would otherwise have remained firmly shut.

Roy Mulcaster's father had been a clergyman. As he grew up, there had never been much money, but his parents had been able to send him to a private school. The public school in the rundown rural area where his father worked was a very inferior one. When they heard that Lyonesse College offered bursaries to sons of the clergy, it seemed too good a chance to miss. By much sacrificing and planning, they managed to scrape together the money needed for the balance of the fees and for his school clothing and other things required. So Roy became a pupil at Lyonesse. It was a good school of its kind. He was happy there and received a good education. It was exclusively a boarding school. It had fine buildings, a beautiful chapel, a well-stocked library, and spacious grounds and playing fields. There was a certain amount of invested endowment, but the money to pay for most of its day-to-day operation had to come from the fees. Although the directors could manage to take a few pupils, such as Roy, for reduced fees, they were obliged to set the charges for the remainder at so high a figure that, without any real desire for it, Lyonesse College was inevitably a school for rich men's sons. All the boys were treated exactly the same and Roy suffered no kind of embarrassment from the inferior financial position of his parents. But, through attending this school, his tastes were enlarged, especially as he grew older. The occasional visits to the homes of school friends during the vacations opened his eyes to ways of luxurious living of which he had never dreamed before.

The process continued at college. Roy had decided to become

a doctor. His real academic ability had won him certain bursaries; he managed to find the remainder of the money by means of summer jobs and midweek evening work during term time in a local cafeteria. He was obliged, of course, to live away from home and so took up residence in the house of his fraternity. Immediately he had arrived in college, he had been elected to the fraternity to which most of the former pupils of Lyonesse College belonged. The way of life in the fraternity house was an expensive one. The young men were well-to-do. They surrounded themselves with the good things to which their families were accustomed. Roy kept his head and knew that most of this was beyond his reach. But he acquired a knowledge of and a taste for a good wine, a well-chosen meal, a vintage brandy, and a fine cigar.

The college years passed, so did the period of interning, and at last Dr. Roy Mulcaster was free to set up a practice on his own. As his income steadily increased, he set out to indulge the educated tastes in good food and drink that had been frustrated up to now. He joined a club famous for its cuisine. He began to stock a cellar of his own with a few dozen of the best years of different wines. He became knowledgeable about sauces and cheeses. His choice imported cigars were kept in a special humidor. He read several books about the cooking of fish and poultry. His friends laughed a little at him but, although Roy would smile back, in fact he was not really amused. He had found a satisfying and engrossing interest. It began to leave him less and less time for other things.

He was not an irreligious man. His parents had given him good training at home and, at Lyonesse College, religious instruction had been a normal part of the school program. Some of the chapel services had affected him deeply. Medical students are not noted for piety. The usual strong doses of science and anatomy had turned most of his contemporaries in medical school into genially bawdy agnostics. But Roy had held firm to the faith of his boyhood. Throughout his college career, he had attended church pretty regularly. When he set up in practice for himself, he transferred to the church nearest to him. But, from

that point, things went backward. He found few at the church
who cared to share his absorbing interest in refined and cultured
living. On a few occasions, he invited his rector and other church
acquaintances to dinner. But it was evident that the finer points
of his hospitality were lost upon them. Their return invitations
were not enjoyable. The unskillful efforts of a busy housewife
were not Roy's idea of a proper dinner. No one seemed prepared to give the serious attention that these matters require.
During the second year of his membership there, the rector decided to hold a parish harvest supper. With much misgiving Roy
attended and found himself confronted with canned soup, boiled
beef, pumpkin pie, and instant coffee. He was revolted. Worse
still, there crept into his heart a contempt for his fellow parishioners who were happily consuming the unimaginative food that
was placed before them. He did not recognize it as such, but
it was a turning point. The smell of cooking that hung about
the church basement, next morning after service, was distasteful
to him. It contrasted unfavorably with the spotless and odorless
dining room at the Gourmet Club. To himself and to others,
Roy gave different reasons for what now gradually began to
happen. When a man is wanting an excuse to cut himself off
from the Church, there are always plenty to be found. His at-
tendances became less regular, his involvement in parish life less
enthusiastic, and in a year or two he had drifted away almost
completely from living contact with the Church. He had found
other things to interest him instead. What the devil could not
achieve through direct assault at medical school, he managed to
bring about through fastidiousness, overrefinement, and a pre-
occupation with the affairs of the palate. A soul had been caught
by gluttony.

In Dante's *Purgatorio* (Canto 23), the prayer of penitence
given for the gluttonous to say is those words which nowadays
begin the Episcopal daily services of Morning and Evening
Prayer. They are taken from Psalm 51. "O Lord, open thou my
lips, and my mouth shall show forth thy praise." It is an appropriate reminder that the mouth was made for other things
besides eating and drinking. The evil of gluttony lies in the way

it exalts the body at the expense of the spirit. It produces a materialistic outlook, impatient of religion and the things of the soul.

The contrary virtue to gluttony is temperance. The good things of the world—including good food and drink—are there for us to enjoy, and it is right to enjoy them with a thankful heart. It is a question of degree, of balance, of proportion. The puritan answer is withdrawal and abstinence; but this is not the traditionally Christian attitude. The characteristic response of the Christian is a healthy and wholehearted enjoyment, coupled with praise and gratitude to God the giver.

He causeth the grass to grow for the cattle and herb for the service of man: that he may bring food out of the earth.
And wine that maketh glad the heart of man, and oil to make his face to shine, and bread which strengtheneth man's heart. . . .
O Lord, how manifold are thy works! In wisdom hast thou made them all: the earth is full of thy riches.

Psalm 104:14-15, 24

All sin is a perversion of what is good, an abuse of what is wholesome, a misuse of what is natural. Gluttony is no exception. The answer to it is not to run to excess in the opposite direction as the puritan does. We speak of overindulgence in alcohol or the misuse of the pleasures of the table, and this suggests that there is a right and proper use of these things. We cannot speak of overindulgence in theft or the misuse of murder. These things are wrong in themselves and therefore have no proper use at all. The fact that the enjoyment of food and drink can be abused does not mean that it is wrong when used properly. The true answer to gluttony is not abstinence but temperate use and controlled enjoyment.

Temperance is achieved by self-control, which, for the Christian, must mean God-control. The best road to this is by means of fasting. It is to be expected that a fat and self-indulgent society such as ours should make light of fasting. Few people think seriously about it at all. But this only shows our spiritual immaturity. The complete self-control at which the Christian should aim is practically impossible without fasting in some form.

Fasting as a means of asserting the supremacy of the spirit over the body has been used and valued by religious men for centuries. It was commonly used in Old Testament times and is well understood today in other religions besides the Christian. In view of the frequent references to it in the New Testament, it is odd that so many modern Christians discount it. We read that our Lord himself fasted, which one might suppose would be recommendation enough for any of his followers. In fact, he told his disciples that deep spiritual power was impossible without it.

It is apparent that before coming to some important decision, the early Christians added the act of fasting to their prayers for guidance.

As they ministered to the Lord and fasted, the Holy Ghost said, Separate me Barnabas and Saul for the work whereunto I have called them. And when they had fasted and prayed, and laid their hands on them, they sent them away.

Acts 13:2-3

And when they had ordained them elders in every church, and had prayed with fasting, they commended them to the Lord, on whom they believed.

Acts 14:23

Fasting was an accepted discipline undertaken by the early Christians, at certain seasons, from time to time, and it has been continued within the Church ever since. Devout people have found that there is great spiritual value in marking all Fridays of the year with some act of bodily self-denial. It helps to remind us that it was on a Friday that the dear Lord died to save us. This small act of abstinence from a favorite food helps to recall what day it is and, as the day runs it course, will provide us with occasions when we can quietly lift up our heart to the Christ who on this day was crucified for us. The small effort of self-denial also helps to establish that control of the bodily desires that arms us against gluttony. The season of Lent is another traditional time for undertaking special rules of bodily self-discipline. By such means, the soul gains a mastery over that tricky partner, the body, to which it is tied for good or evil. A person who makes a regular and sensible use of fasting has at hand a proved and powerful help toward temperance and self-control and a defense against self-indulgence and gluttony.

"Blessed are they that hunger and thirst after righteousness," said Jesus, "for they shall be filled." For the ordinary man it is sufficient to satisfy one's own moral standards or to approximate to those accepted by contemporary society. But our Lord sets out a higher standard than this. The metaphor of thirst was a very real and vital one in Palestine. It calls up the idea of the most consuming desire that a man can feel. Just as hunger and thirst are signs of a healthy body, so their spiritual counterparts are the signs of a healthy soul.

It is these spiritual desires that gluttony so quickly deadens. There is an apocryphal saying of Jesus which does not appear in any of the Four Gospels, but which might well have been truly said by him. "I stood in the midst of the world, and in the flesh was I seen of men: and I found all men drunken, and none found I athirst."

Our Lord was so consumed with zeal for his Father's business that we read how, again and again, it lifted him above the need and desire for physical food. On one occasion, he and his disciples were walking north from Judea, through Samaria, to Galilee. They came to Sychar and there the disciples left him sitting by the well while they went into the city to buy food. Presently, a Samaritan woman came to draw water and Jesus asked her for a drink. They fell into a conversation that was of the greatest importance for her and ended in her conversion. At last, the disciples returned, bringing the food they had bought. But Jesus was no longer hungry. He had had food, he told them, which they didn't know about. The disciples wondered to each other whether anyone else had given him something to eat. Jesus said: "My food is to do the will of him that sent me and to finish his work." The successful wrestling for the woman's soul had so refreshed him that he had forgotten his hunger. It was a complete reversal of the sin of gluttony. The things of the spirit were of far greater importance to him than the promptings of the body.

Occasionally we meet people who take such a keen delight in doing something that we say that "it is meat and drink" to them. Our Lord says that those who desire righteousness in that way will not miss being filled. This is not something which we can do for ourselves, however. We can never stand right with God by our own deserving. But if righteousness is the supreme object of our desire; if we look upon it as the chief end and intention of our lives; if we accept it as God's word of promise for us; then God accounts it ours already and he will make it ours indeed in the end.

SCRIPTURE

Woe unto them that rise up early in the morning that they may follow strong drink; that continue until night, till wine inflame them.

Isaiah 5:11

Many walk, of whom I have told you often, and now tell you even weeping, that they are the enemies of the cross of Christ; whose end is destruction, whose God is their belly, and whose glory is in their shame, who mind earthly things.

Philippians 3:18-19

All things are lawful unto me, but all things are not expedient: all things are lawful for me, but I will not be brought under the power of any. Meats for the belly, and the belly for meats; but God shall destroy both it and them.

I Corinthians 6:12-13

And every man that striveth for the mastery is temperate in all things. Now they do it to obtain a corruptible crown; but we are incorruptible. I therefore so run, not as uncertainly; so fight I, not as one that beateth the air: But I keep under my body, and bring it into subjection.

I Corinthians 9:25-27

PRAYERS

O Merciful Lord, God, who hast vouchsafed to feed us, thy unworthy creatures, with that Bread which came down from heaven and giveth life unto the soul, so strengthen and sustain me by thy most gracious gifts, that I may resist all the temptations to fleshly self-indulgence, and, walking in the way of thy commandments, may glorify thy holy Name; through Jesus Christ our Lord. Amen.

O Lord, who for our sake didst fast forty days and forty nights: Give us grace to use such abstinence that, our flesh being subdued to the Spirit, we may ever obey thy godly motions in righteousness and true holiness; to thy honor and glory who livest and reignest with the Father and the Holy Ghost, one God world without end. Amen.

> Dear Master, in whose life I see
> All I desire but fail to be,
> Let thy clear light for ever shine,
> To shame and guide this life of mine.
>
> Though what I dream and what I do
> In my poor days are always two,
> Help me, oppressed by things undone,
> O Thou, whose dreams and deeds are one.

Eternal God, who by thy holy breath of power makest us a new creation for thyself, we beseech thee to preserve what thou hast created, and to consecrate what thou hast cleansed; that by thy grace we may be found in that form, the thought of which ever dwells with thee, and which thou by thy Spirit can fulfill in us.

Chapter 9

LUST

After Gluttony cometh Lechery, for these two sinnes be so near cousins, that oft time they will not separate—This cursed sinne annoyeth grievously them that it haunts; and first to the soule, for he obligeth it to sinne and to pain of death—and to the body, for it drieth him, and wasteth and ruineth him.

Chaucer, *Canterbury Tales*

The Contrary Virtue to Lust is Chastity

Blessed are the pure in heart

LUST may be defined as wholly selfish sexual desire. No doubt for biological reasons, so that the race may continue, the sex act is a deeply pleasurable one. In the course of it, a man and a woman give and derive profound satisfaction and enjoyment. This is as God meant it to be, and is entirely right and wholesome. But, as a consequence of the Fall, each human being has been thrown inward upon himself and has become imprisoned within the iron ring of self. As a result, there is always a tendency to regard the other partner in sexual intercourse merely as one through whom to derive pleasure. This is to dehumanize the sex act. It is to treat another human being as a thing. The sex urge can thus become introverted and can degenerate into lust. Love has been well defined as the relationship that treats people as persons. Lust treats people as things.

Larry had never been very popular at school. He had been reasonably athletic and had made about average grades all along, but there had always been something about him which had prompted a vague dislike. For one thing, there was a strain of cruelty in him, which came out in his treatment of smaller boys and animals. Although several boys had joined in the business of tying firecrackers to the janitor's cat's tail, when they saw the animal's resultant terror, the others had been secretly ashamed. Only Larry had continued to find it amusing.

As they grew older, most of them experimented sexually on themselves and others and, at a slightly later stage, carried out such investigations of the female body as their girl friends could be persuaded to allow. But for most, these fumbling experiences were accompanied by puppy-love attachment at the same time. The girl was an object of desire certainly, but she was also the lady love of adolescent romanticism. Another reason why Larry was unpopular was that he was the first to be openly derisive of any such softer or romantic side to these affairs. He had picked up a few cynical phrases to describe them, and in consequence made the others feel both guilty and immature at the same time. He himself boasted that he went out with a girl for one thing only and the sooner he made it the better. He was already learning to dehumanize the opposite sex.

After graduation from high school, he went to work for his

uncle who had a wholesale hardware distributing business. He put Larry on the road as a representative. He did well. The work did not call for much intelligence and Larry quickly mastered the technical details. He was not shy. He could meet people and make his pitch clearly and successfully. He became well-established in a fair-sized territory.

He soon struck up an acquaintance with likely young women in several neighborhoods. He preferred the amateur to the professional. So long as he did not have to waste too much time in reaching attainment, Larry enjoyed the process of seduction. It gave him a feeling of power. It often gratified his desire for cruelty. About the young women themselves he cared very little. He had a harsh word for them. He called them his crows.

He was in no hurry to get married. Why should he? he would ask. He was doing fine as it was. A wife put the bite on you for a permanent meal ticket but you could tell a crow to beat it whenever you wanted. When he was in his late thirties, however, he took the step. She was a pretty little redhead, fifteen years younger than he was, and the daughter of one of his firm's best customers. Larry considered it a very suitable match. For some time, although he did not admit it even to himself, he had not found twenty-year-old girls as responsive to his advances as they once had been.

At first, Sylvia came up to his highest expectations. Larry was an accomplished performer and they both greatly enjoyed the process of her education. But it was not in his character to be content with one woman for long. He was not really capable of love at all, in the proper sense of the word. Within the first year, he had begun to think it not worthwhile to drive two hundred miles home, at the end of a business trip. There were always willing girls to be found if a man knew where to look. Sylvia was a pretty enough little thing to be sure, but, when it came to that, all women look the same in the dark.

There is no need to dwell on the heartache and sorrow that followed during the next few years. Eventually, Sylvia suspected; presently she knew for certain. There were scenes of anger, of cynicism, of sentimental reconciliation; they were repeated many times. Gradually mutual trust and affection were lost completely. For the sake of the children who had arrived by this time, they did not separate; Larry saw no need to. The marriage settled down into a bickering and nagging dreariness from which the ecstasy of passion and the warmth of mutual affection were both missing. All that marriage is supposed to mean, all that it can in fact truly come to mean, had been lost and ruined by lust.

It has often been pointed out that our age is one where visual stimulation to lust is offered continually on all sides. In movie, television, and magazine advertising, the same old theme shrieks at us. The picture of a pneumatically bosomed young woman may come to be regarded in later generations as the typical symbol of our period. This would not be so bad if it indicated a frank and healthy interest in what is naturally a matter of great importance to everyone. Along with this curious obsession with secondhand visual sex, however, there goes an inability to be natural about it in other ways also.

The stripteaser is the product of a civilization that has lost the way to natural sex. For many men the nasty story compensates for their own sexual frustration. Our female fashions are so revealing and seductive that they create scandal in other and more decorous countries. Yet the proportion of frigid women in our civilization is said to be very high. Our second-rate writers have long since discovered that a few raw and juicy passages are what sell books. In some novels, you can hear the cumbersome wheels of the author's imagination creaking round as he decides that by now the time has come for another bed-room scene or a fast pass in the hayloft. We like to read about irregular sex. We are a sexy people, and yet at the same time we are inhibited about it. The obsession is sly and furtive; it does not issue out into healthy natural action. We are rather like old men impotently savoring the matter at second hand.

Against such a background, it is not easy to avoid that warped view of the matter, which leads into lust, nor to recapture the true view, which leads to chaste love and personal fulfillment.

The impulse to lust is of two kinds: the physical and the mental. The physical impulse should not be underestimated. It is always a force to be reckoned with, especially in adolescence. But a great deal of nonsense is talked about its invincibility. It is neither unhealthy nor impossible to control and sublimate it. Many a young man has given in to lust because he has been told that it is impossible not to do so, or because of vague ideas that chastity is harmful. Neither of these theories is true. Sensible diet, coupled with healthy recreation and exercise, helps to reduce the physical urge. But a young person who indulges in overrich food and much alcohol, and who takes no regular exercise, is making sexual self-control unnecessarily difficult for himself.

Much more important is the mental impulse. This is the more powerful of the two, because if the mind is free from lust, the bodily craving will either not arise at all or, if it does arise, will be kept in check. Each individual's personal struggle for purity is fought, and won or lost, in the mind. As with physical diet, so with mental diet, sensible discretion must be used. The person who feeds his mind on garbage is asking for trouble. Our character is dyed the color of its thoughts. Some people carry a favorite lustful image in the mind, and bring it out from time to time in order to make a kind of evil meditation on it. If such a person's mind becomes unoccupied at any time, lustful imaginings are likely to take possession of it.

"Where your treasure is, there will your heart be also." If I love Heaven, I think readily of heavenly things. If I love the world, I take pleasure in the delights of the world, and grieve at its troubles. If I love my body, my imagination dwells often on the things of the body—For whatever things I love, it is of these that I am eager to speak and hear, and I have these interests always at heart.

Thomas à Kempis (*Imitation,* Bk. III, chap. 48)

Writers who take for granted a low level of sexual morality in books that pretend to portray the behavior of ordinary people have a great deal to answer for. They always claim, of course (or their publishers claim for them), that they are "frank," "stark," or "realist" and above all "not puritanical." But the harm they do is widespread. In his sensitive relating of the love affair between Willie and May which forms part of his book, *The Caine Mutiny*, Herman Wouk has well described the influence of this type of writing.

It was all of a long winter night before Willie returned to his own room, and sank into an armchair in an excess of stupefied pleasure, still thinking with joy of his last glimpse of May, enchanting in her simple white nightdress, with her red hair tumbled on her bare shoulders, smiling up at him as he closed her door. It was a perfectly satisfying picture, and he had no way of knowing that in her room below, May was crouched in a chair, shivering and crying.

It was a familiar story: the young man back from the war, eager for his love, impatient of the cautious rules of peace time; his girl, no less eager for him, and ready to do anything to make him happy; and so, good-bye rules! Willie had never tried to force May to yield to him. He had feared the entanglement more than he wanted this last intimacy, and their relationship had been full of sweetness without it. Nor did he force her this night. It happened; and it happened the more easily because they had both read lots of books which dismissed the rules as pretty primitive taboos and asserted that all morals were relative to time and place. Willie, floating in a daze of well being, was certain at this moment that the books contained true wisdom. May, for some reason, wasn't so sure. Anyway, the deed was done.

The resulting damage to the relationship between Willie and May is well described as the story continues. Although a happy ending is hinted at toward the end of the book, much bitter pain and misunderstanding could have been spared to them in the meantime.

Writers of the kind that Wouk criticizes make the calm assumption that the battle is already decided against purity by all intelligent people. They do not argue the matter, or try to draw their action and characters from real life where these issues must be worked out in the lives of men and women. Instead, they go over to the side that is fashionable at the moment and that will pay best, and so they make rape and fornication seem smart and attractive. (A few years of pastoral work would show them the bitterness and heartbreak which are in fact the fruits of the behavior they portray so gaily.)

The drugstore book counter seems to sell a high percentage of its wares on this basis. It is amusing to notice how many books of blameless rectitude are disguised with glaring pictorial jackets which promise something quite different from the real contents. The purchaser is deceived into buying under false pretenses. He spends his fifty cents for a paperback with a lurid cover, hoping for some enjoyable pornography, only to find himself fobbed off with a text of unrelieved morality. It is yet another illustration of our warped attitude to sex that the best way to sell a book is apparently to display it on the shelf marked "lust."

"No girl has ever been seduced by a book." This witty remark by Mayor James J. Walker has served as a substitute for thought in the minds of many people since it was made. The issue cannot be dismissed so easily. Even good literature can be dangerous and can provide fuel to the flames of prurience. The lustful mind will feed upon anything. To some people, the nude will always be nothing more than an undressed woman.

Should such dangerous books be banned then? To ban them is to deprive the reader with an adult mind of some excellent literature, which he is surely entitled to read if he wishes. To allow them to be published is to take a chance that the general reading public will be more balanced and mature than in fact they are likely to prove. The recent case in England of D. H. Lawrence's *Lady Chatterley's Lover* is a good example. Comparatively few people knew much about it before the trial, but the evidence made it clear that here was a sexually exciting book. When permission was given to print it, a well-known paperback publishing firm rushed four million copies into print and expected to sell them all without difficulty. Were there really four million serious students of literature waiting for it?

The two sides of this contentious argument are parallel to the two views that people take about liquor. One party advocates prohibition and total abstinence in order to protect the weaker brethren who would misuse it. The other urges a bold attempt to use in a right and mature manner something that can certainly be abused. Both sides have good arguments in their favor. To adopt either policy is to do harm, one way or the other. On balance, it would seem that at the moment, liberty has passed into license, and many of our books and magazines could do with a drastic cleanup. This will not happen, of course, except through the pressure of public opinion. In a matter like this, a nation gets roughly what it really wants.

The human race has fallen into a dilemma over sex but there is no solution along the lines of a naturalistic attitude to it, as some people try to advocate. Men are not animals and are not able to behave as such without doing deep violence to their personalities. There is more to human love than going on heat. The naturalistic solution is a superficial and a sentimental one. Rousseau's concept of the happy and innocent savage was a mirage. No such person ever existed. This matter of sex is everywhere surrounded with the sense of guilt and shame which in turn gives rise to elaborate taboos, varying from tribe to tribe. The happy, animal-like, innocent, carefree savage is a figment of the imagination.

We are more than bodies and yet we have bodies. Here is the difficulty. Attempts are often made to solve it by treating human beings either as if they had no bodies at all, or as if they were nothing but bodies. Both these views of the nature of man are inadequate and in fact lead to no solution at all. Man is a creature who is at once physical and spiritual; he shares some of his qualities with the rest of the animal creation but he also possesses unique spiritual attributes and capabilities. He is neither all animal nor all spiritual. He is both at the same time. The composition of water gives us an analogy. Two elements, hydrogen and oxygen, quite different from each other, when combined in the right proportions, bring into being a third substance, water, with its own characteristics clearly differentiating it from either of the other two which make it up. So it is with man. He is not an animal merely, nor is he a spiritual being merely. If we try to separate these two parts of him, even in thought, we are no longer thinking of man as he really is.

Lust causes a person to act as if his body were all there is of him. He buys a temporary pleasure at the price of doing violence to his true nature, sometimes with deep and lasting

damage to his personality as a result. It is a terrible example
of the truth that all sin is an attempt to get out of life something which God has not put into it, something which in fact is not
really there at all. We clutch it to us because it seems to promise
happiness; but the pretty bubble breaks, and we find that it was
filled with stale air.

What we do with our bodies has a profound influence upon
our inmost being. The body is a holy thing. St. Paul called it a
temple of the Holy Spirit who animates it and dwells within
it. It is rather like a church building, and should be treated
reverently for much the same reason. This is why all misuse
of the body is wrong. To use it for the purposes of lust is a
defilement both of the body itself, and of the person who permits
the defilement.

> This is not Love? The action is the same;
> The highest passion seeks but this same end.
> May I know Love hereafter? On my wedding night
> Between my bride's pale purity and me,
> Between her pouting lips and mine, that search
> To wake her sleeping woman's nature there,
> Shall not rise up the image of this thing,
> These cold lips tired of kisses, and that sex
> Aweary of its function?

The contrary virtue to lust is chastity. People who would like
to combine lust and respectability talk a great deal of nonsense
about this subject. Because lust is a very popular sin, chastity is
often made to appear a very unattractive virtue. It is portrayed
as an anemic, colorless, unmanly kind of affair, even rather
ludicrous and contemptible. In his novel, *War and Peace*, Tol-
stoy has drawn a remarkable picture of a profligate rake in the
character of Anatole Kuragin. He points out that such men,
whom he rightly describes as male Magdalenes, have a secret
feeling of innocence similar to that which female Magdalenes
have, and based on the same hope of forgiveness. "All will be
forgiven her, for she loved much," said our Lord. All will be
forgiven me, thinks her male counterpart, for I have enjoyed

much. God will no doubt be indulgent. As a result he harbors a contempt for the chaste man who has missed his opportunities for fun through timid scrupulosity.

But chastity is not a denial of passion. It has been well defined as "having the body in the soul's keeping." It holds the right priorities. The body is a good servant but a bad master. The sins of lust are not natural to man. They are a violation of his true nature. Impurity is, in the strictest sense of the word, "abnormal" not because it is uncommon (unfortunately it is not) but because it violates the law of man's being. True manliness consists in subduing the desires to the control of the will. Christian asceticism aims not at annihilating such desires but at reducing them to order. When this is achieved, the course of love can flow deeply and surely. The bodily act between husband and wife becomes sacramental of their whole lifelong relationship with each other. Lust divides, coarsens, and dehumanizes. Chaste love unites and uplifts, and makes two people more richly human than they were before.

One of the consequences of man's rejection of God's plan for him was that the bond between man and woman was seriously impaired. They became self-conscious in the presence of each other and guilt entered in as a barrier between them. In Christian marriage, there can take place a reversal of what happened when mankind rebelled against God. As a consequence of that rebellion, each person was thrown inward upon himself or herself, and became imprisoned within the iron ring of self. Christian marriage provides a situation where this can begin to be undone. Sin, shame, guilt, selfishness, and pride all pervert and spoil the relation of the sexes; but, in Christian marriage, these damaging factors can be at their minimum, or can even be transcended. The sense of shame cannot be erased by trying to acquire a naturalistic attitude to sex. Men are not animals and they cannot find a solution for their sexual dilemma in trying to act as if they were. But married love, protected by the marriage vows, can provide the path toward a solution. Married love involves much more than the first flowering of youthful passion, although that has its rightful place. It involves the whole sweep of a man's and a woman's life together, the shared experiences of happy times and unhappy times, the coming of children, the tending of them at the different stages of their growing-up, the years of middle age together, and finally the shared old age, full of mutual memories and perhaps with grand-children to brighten and complete it. Although they cannot fully comprehend it at the time, this is what a young couple are delivering themselves into, when they come starry-eyed to the clergyman to make arrangements for their wedding. Christian marriage, and the deep and abiding love made possible within it, are a school of holiness and spiritual maturity.

"Blessed are the pure in heart," said Jesus, "for they shall see God." The Jews of his day had many elaborate rules to safeguard ritual purity. The laws of Moses had by his time been so expanded and amplified that almost every conceivable action had received its due consideration and the ritually correct safe-guards had been established to surround it. If our Lord had said simply: "Blessed are the pure," his hearers would have thought that he was merely endorsing the external and ritual purity demanded by the law. But he added "in heart." He was concerned to guard against a merely external conception of purity. It is not what goes into a man's stomach that defiles him, but what comes out of his heart. So the seat of purity is not in outward observances. It lies deep within the personality. St. Peter's vision at Joppa showed the Church that the old distinction between the ritually clean and the ritually unclean had been done away in Christ. In Christ, everything is clean and sacred. Nothing is unclean and profane of itself; it only becomes so for the person who defiles it by his own sinful attitude.

As this Beatitude points out, then, true purity is not an external thing. It is "of the heart." The phrase "pure in heart" might almost be translated "single hearted." Our Lord was speaking of the same truth when he said: "The light of the body is the eye; if therefore thine eye be single, thy whole body shall be full of light." The single eye is the eye that sees the thing it looks at because it is not looking at so many other things at the same time. Indeed this Beatitude could almost be reversed. "Blessed are they that see God, for they shall be pure."

The deepest insights of psychology have taught us that the most successful recipe for a happy and fulfilled life is to lose oneself in something greater than oneself. Man discovers that conscious efforts in the direction of self-seeking are strangely self-frustrating. Ambition costs us friends; power corrupts those who wield it; wealth brings the curse of Midas; sexual excess ends in secret disgust. This should come as no surprise to the followers of him who said: "Whosoever would save his life shall lose it; and whosoever shall lose his life for my sake and the gospel's shall save it."

Man's salvation lies in losing himself in something greater than himself, which can liberate him for effective living. Yet he finds self-love the hardest thing in the world to surrender. The most fortunate people are those who are caught up in an absorbing enthusiasm or consuming devotion so that self is forgotten. But a man cannot do this for himself. He can put himself in the way of it but cannot deliberately cause himself to be thus liberated. Which is another way of saying that a man cannot save himself but can only be saved.

One of the most searching books of that great Scandinavian religious giant, Søren Kierkegaard, is entitled, *Purity of Heart Is to Will One Thing*. The price of it is commitment, loyalty, and readiness to endure everything that may be required, to hold nothing back. Those whom God grants to see him in this way find purity of heart; and purity of heart ("to will one thing") brings the soul to where, without other things coming between and hiding him from our sight, we may see God and be satisfied.

SCRIPTURE

Now the body is not for fornication but for the Lord; and the Lord for the body. . . . Know ye not that your bodies are the members of Christ? Shall I then take the members of Christ, and make them the members of an harlot? God forbid. What? Know ye not that he which is joined to an harlot is one body? For two, saith he, shall be one flesh. Flee fornication. Every sin that a man doeth is without the body; but he that committeth fornication sinneth against his own body. What? Know ye not that your body is the temple of the Holy Ghost which is in you, and ye are not your own. For ye are bought with a price. Therefore glorify God in your body, and in your spirit, which are God's.

1 Corinthians 6:13, 15-20

Finally, brethren, whatsoever things are true, whatsoever things are honest, whatsoever things are just, whatsoever things are pure, whatsoever things are lovely, whatsoever things are of good report; if there be any virtue, and if there be any praise, think on these things.

Philippians 4:8

Who shall ascend into the hill of the Lord? Or who shall stand in his holy place? Even he that hath clean hands and a pure heart.

Psalm 24:3-4

PRAYERS

Purify me, O Lord, with the fire of thy Holy Spirit, that I may serve thee with a chaste body and please thee with a pure mind, through Jesus Christ our Lord. Amen.

O holy and immaculate Jesus, who wast born of a pure Virgin, cleanse me, I pray thee, from all filthiness of flesh and spirit. Suffer me at no time to pollute my body, which is the temple of the Holy Ghost, with any uncleanness; and enable me to keep my heart with all diligence, so that no unchaste thoughts may be harbored there; but that, being pure and undefiled in both body and soul, I may glorify thee here, and be glorified with thee hereafter, who livest and reignest with the Father and the Holy Spirit, one God world without end. Amen.

Almighty God, who seest that we have no power of ourselves to help ourselves. Keep us both outwardly in our bodies, and inwardly in our souls; that we may be defended from all adversities which may happen to the body, and from all evil thoughts which may assault and hurt the soul; through Jesus Christ our Lord. Amen.

Chapter 10

THE WAY BACK

And when he came to himself, he said: I will arise and go to my father, and will say unto him, Father I have sinned against heaven, and before thee, and am no more worthy to be called thy son. . . . And he arose, and came to his father.

The Parable of the Prodigal Son

WHEN we fall into sin, there is a way back for us if we choose to take it. This book is not the place for a long and detailed theological discussion of how this has been made possible for us. It was achieved by the coming of God's Son and by his death and resurrection for our sake. There are only two facts about this that I want to mention here. First: Only God could do it. It was his doing, not ours. Second: It was immensely costly for him.

One of the worst things about sin, as we all know from our own experience, is that every time a person sins in some way, he is that much more likely to do it again in similar circumstances. Human nature is such that a man's future behavior is very much influenced by what his past behavior has been. Indeed, the phrase "Let's do it again" might be taken as the motto of the whole human race. We tend always to repeat what we have done before. So, once sin had entered into the situation, it was not possible for man to regain the lost ground. Children inherited a weakened moral character from their parents. They grew up in a society where disobedience to God had become universal. The very atmosphere, as it were, was contaminated. Everyone was infected by the common contagion and contributed his share to infecting others with it.

And worse than this. Their sin so weakened men's character and blinded their understanding that they were no longer able to perceive the evil state into which they had fallen. There are some men who, as they become more and more drunk, become also more and more persuaded that they are possessed of profound and important truths. Sin worked in mankind in much the same way. Intoxicated and beguiled by it, men could no longer discern spiritual reality. Like lost travelers in the desert, they mistook mirages for wells and looked for happiness in places where it cannot possibly be found. It is worth remembering that sin is the one human experience about which it is true to say that the more you experience it, the less you really know about it. Holiness understands sin, but sin understands neither itself nor holiness; just as waking understands sleeping, but sleeping does not understand what it is to be awake, or to be asleep. Each of the seven root sins that we have considered in this book is a path down which men have looked for happiness but have not found it.

Men were deceived and misled because of their sin, and so could never hope to find the way back without help from outside; they had become weakened in their very nature and so could not in fact live holy lives even if they wanted to; they had disobeyed God and guilt had entered in to spoil the relationship between him and them. It was to meet and redeem this situation that Christ came, for only God himself could do what needed to be done. The fact that the way is now open for us to return to him is in no sense our doing.

> Light looked down and beheld Darkness
>> "Thither will I go," said Light.
> Peace looked down and beheld War,
>> "Thither will I go," said Peace.
> Love looked down and beheld Hatred
>> "Thither will I go," said Love.
> So came Light and shone;
> So came Peace and gave rest;
> So came Love and brought life;
> And the Word was made Flesh, and dwelt among us.
>> Laurence Housman

He came from God. He was God. From start to finish, the whole achievement was something that God did on our behalf, but without our assistance. In him, God acted. In him, the eternal world of God broke in upon our little world of time and space. Our redemption was won by supernatural means, in the strictest sense of those words; the means by which it was accomplished were not of this world.

The early days of the last century were a time of new religions put forward as substitutes for Christianity. They were carefully rational, and moral, and socially relevant, and non-institutional, and unsupernatural, and everything else that Christianity was supposed not to be. But somehow they failed to catch on. The leader of one of them complained to Talleyrand, the great French statesman who was himself no friend of the Church, that he could not make many converts. "What would your Excellency advise?" he asked. "I should recommend you," said Talleyrand, "to be crucified and to rise again the third day."

> He only could unlock the gate
> Of heaven, and let us in.

But that was not done easily. Archbishop Söderblom has well said: "God reached into the world to save man and, in doing so, his hand was grievously bruised." If you love someone, he has the power to hurt you by his indifference and neglect. The more deeply you love him, the more deeply it is in his power to hurt you. The extraordinary truth is that God loved us unlovely men with an infinite love that knew no bounds, and so we had the power to hurt him infinitely. When he came to save us, we exercised this power with vicious willfulness. God's Son nailed to a cross is the eternal sign of the price that we made him pay.

It has been a true instinct which has led Christians to choose the cross as the symbol of their faith. There were other symbols that might have been chosen: the manger, the carpenter's bench, the Holy Grail, the empty tomb. All of these would have expressed profound truths about who Christ is and what he came to do. But, among all the leaders of the world, Christ is preeminently he who was crucified. Christians saw from the first that the cross went to the heart of the matter for it was supremely there that the work of our redemption was accomplished.

> Sing, my tongue, the glorious battle
>   Sing the ending of the fray;
> Now above the Cross, the trophy,
>   Sound the loud triumphant lay;
> Tell how Christ, the world's redeemer,
>   As a Victim won the day.

There is a legend about a rich merchant who had come to his last sickness. As he lay in bed one night, he slept and dreamed that he had arrived at the Last Judgment. Before him was a huge pair of scales. On one side the devils were piling up all the things he had done wrong during his life, while on the other side the angels were placing what good things he had done and what merit he had acquired during his time on earth. The pile on the left side was heavy enough certainly; but he had been a good man and there was much that could be placed to his credit. On the right side of the scales, the angels placed his good deeds, his gifts to the Church and to the poor, his acts of Communion, his prayers. But when all was placed on the scales, to his horror the merchant saw them begin to tip in the wrong direction. In his dream, he cried out, "Lord, save me." There was a small metallic sound and, as he looked, a nail was dropped into the right-hand scale. It was followed by another, and by a third; and the balance changed over to the other side. There is no man whose good deeds will outweigh his sins; but there is also no one whose sins are beyond the forgiveness wrought by the Passion of God's Son.

It is for each individual soul to allow this to become true for him.

> Though Christ in Bethlehem
> A thousand times were born,
> Unless He's born in thee,
> He was never born at all.

By his redeeming power, Christ takes us up into something greater than ourselves and so enables us to rise to heights of which we would be otherwise quite incapable. An analogy can be drawn from the theater. The plays of a writer like Shakespeare provide the great actors with their supreme opportunity and call from them better work than they could otherwise achieve. We may compare such performances to the achievements of the saints. But, more than this, the plays of Shakespeare redeem the bad actor. So long as he is speaking that imcomparable verse with any kind of success at all, he is lifted for the moment beyond his own incompetence; but give him a cheap, slick play and his own poor quality becomes immediately apparent. So, for us ordinary souls, to be forgiven and redeemed, to be caught up by Christ into his risen and ascended life, means that like the poor actor in the great play, even we can begin to share in a splendor that is not our own.

The means to this is repentance, which Jeremy Taylor calls "a plank after shipwreck." There is a good deal more to repentance than many people realize. It has four parts: confession, contrition, reparation, amendment. In case you should be thinking that this is only adding unnecessary and involved complications to a simple thing, let us take an everyday example and see what these different parts of repentance mean in practice. Suppose there are two young women who are stenographers in the same office and friendly companions on different occasions outside working hours. For some reason which we won't go into now, perhaps from motives of envy or bad temper, Marjorie tells a malicious and quite unfounded lie defaming her friend. The evil little story goes the rounds of the office and inevitably at last reaches the ears of the other. The friendly relationship between them is instantly broken. Now, suppose Marjorie wants to make it up. This is what the Church would call a desire to repent. There are certain things she must do. She must admit that she really did say these things and that it was not someone else who said them; and that they were quite untrue and without foundation. (This is confession). Then she must be prepared to say that she is now sorry for having acted in this way (contrition) She must put it right if possible (reparation) and take steps for the future to become the kind of person who does not tell malicious lies about her friends (amendment).

When we turn in penitence to God, our repentance must involve these four parts. Sin is often pictured as a disease, or a burden, or a stain, or as an enemy attacking us. All these ideas express truth but they are all too external. Sin is a condition of our own wills, part of our inmost selves. Repentance begins when we are ready to admit this. It was I myself who did this. Unpleasant though it is to admit it, I am apparently the kind of person who does things like this. This sin is part of *me*.

We human beings are self-deceptive. It is a well-known psychological fact that we quickly forget the things which it makes us uncomfortable to remember. A necessary part of earnest repentance therefore is a thorough self-examination. This is something that all Christian people should undertake from time to time. It is quite simple, though unpleasant.

Begin by finding somewhere where you can be quiet and undisturbed. Your church is the best place, but your bedroom will do just as well. Kneel down and ask God the Holy Spirit to help you as you make your examination. Ask him to bring to your remembrance everything that you ought to confess, everything that is spoiling your relationship with him. It may help you to say over one or two of the penitential Psalms or to look at a crucifix or at a picture of Calvary, and to remind yourself of what your share of the world's sin means to the loving heart of God. Then sit up, take a piece of paper, and make a list of the sins you can remember. Some people find it useful to go through the Ten Commandments as a guide. Another good method is to divide your sins into three categories: those against God, those against other people, and those against yourself. Of course, all sins are against God, but some will seem to fall especially into this category. Sins of blasphemy or of mocking at holy things, sins of cowardice about your religion in the presence of its opponents, sins of neglecting prayers and churchgoing. The next category will be the largest for most people. Here you should include all the ways in which you have offended others: sins of dishonesty, cruelty, malice, or impurity (if another person was involved). Then most people will remember sins which have to be included in the third classification. These will be the private sins such as laziness, drunkenness, solitary impurity, and the like. There is no need of course to write out a full account of each sin. Just a word or two will probably be enough. The list is only to ensure that, when the time for confession comes, you will remember to tell God everything, forgetting nothing. When you have completed your list, put it away carefully and keep it for a few days. During this time, ask God each night to keep on helping you to remember all your sins. Then, a few days later, go over the list again, in the same way. You will probably find that you have recalled a few more sins which ought to be included. Remember that not all sins are sins of commission. We offend God not only by the wrong things we do, but by the good things we might have done and have failed to do. If you are like most people, your list will have to contain some of these. The fact that you are reading this book at all means that you have got far beyond the notion that all God requires of us is that we never do anybody else any harm.

> I never cut my neighbor's throat;
> My neighbor's gold I never stole;
> I never spoiled his house and land;
> But God have mercy on my soul!
>
> For I am haunted night and day
> By all the deeds I have not done;
> O unattempted loveliness;
> O costly valor never won.

When your act of self-examination is finished, you are ready for the act of confession. This can be done in one of several ways; but, before we come to consider them, we must first make sure that you are really contrite. Mere self-pity is not contrition, nor is a realization that past opportunities have been wasted, nor regret for past folly. Feelings of this kind are really not much more than a kind of spiritual hangover, a mood of "the morning after." True repentance is always sorrow for the offense done against the love of God. Selfish regret and morbid or sentimental remorse are not contrition, because in these cases, the soul cares little for God but is only sorry for itself as it contemplates its past foolishness. St. Paul pointed out the difference very clearly. "Godly sorrow worketh repentance to salvation; but the sorrow of the world worketh death."

We must probe still a little further. Our emotions depend a great deal upon temperament and physical health. They are not always under our control. What determines the reality of penitence is not how deeply the emotions are stirred but how firmly our will is committed. We can test this by whether we are ready to make whatever reparation is in our power and by how earnestly we intend to take steps against falling into the same sins in the future. Readiness and indeed desire to make reparation is an essential part of true repentance. If a man had swindled a friend out of a sum of money, we would scarcely believe that he was really sorry for what he had done if all he did was say he was sorry but at the same time refused to return the money to his friend. Similarly, an earnest determination to avoid occasions of sin in the future is a necessary mark of true penitence. We would not regard a burglar as being truly penitent if we discovered that he was still carefully maintaining his safecracking equipment in good repair. Repentance must include the sincere desire and intention of turning away from sin and toward God.

> It's not enough to say
>   I'm sorry, and repent,
> But then to go on afterward,
>   Just as you always went.

You have made an honest and complete a self-examination as you can, you are prepared to make whatever reparation is possible, and you earnestly intend to take steps to avoid falling into the same sins again. Now you are ready for the last part of a full repentance. It is not enough just to *be* sorry. We must *say* we are sorry. Christians of different traditions do this in different ways. All the ways are good and all bring God's loving forgiveness into our lives. This is what we are after. The point of forgiveness is not just that we shall feel better and more comfortable with ourselves. It is more than merely a balm to an uneasy conscience. It is the creative power of God coming into us for new life in him.

One way of telling God that we are truly sorry is to go somewhere where we can be quiet, such as in our own room, or in a church, and there to take out our list of sins and go through them before God telling him that we admit before him that we did these things but that we are truly sorry for them and for the grief that we have caused him because of them. Then with his swift and loving mercy, God will meet our repentance with his forgiveness, that forgiveness which his son died on the cross to make possible. We can go away and burn up our list of sins because they are now as though they had never been. This is not something we have earned, not something we have deserved. It is the free gift of God.

Some people find that they cannot quiet their own conscience in this way. They find it helpful to tell their sins to God in the presence of a priest. In the Roman Catholic Church, this is compulsory for everyone at certain times. The Episcopal Church teaches that it is not compulsory, but that everyone may make use of this method of confession if he wishes, and that some people should do so. Other Christian denominations make similar provision. This method of confessing our sins to God is basically the same as the other. The only difference is that a priest hears what we have to say. He is one of God's ordained officers and he represents also the family of God, which we have betrayed and weakened by our faithlessness. We are quite safe with him because no priest ever reveals what he may hear in this way. At the end, he will pronounce the words of God's forgiveness over us and perhaps give us some good advice about how to avoid doing these same sins again. People sometimes seem to think that he is claiming to forgive sins himself; but this is obviously not possible. No one can forgive sins except God. What the priest does is to speak the words for God. For many souls, this helps to bring home the wonder and reality of forgiveness with a special clarity. The work of psychiatrists would be a good deal lighter if more people made use of this method of confession. Sins that are unrepented and unconfessed sometimes sink down deep into the unconscious mind and then fester and breed poison there. After this has gone on for several years, the person is sometimes reduced to such a state that skilled psychiatric treatment becomes necessary. Much of this could often be avoided by private confession in the early stages.

Repentance is the one essential condition upon which God opens to us the treasures of his grace. The message of St. John who came to prepare the way for the Saviour was, "Repent ye, for the Kingdom of Heaven is at hand." When Jesus arrived, his message was the same, "Repent ye and believe the gospel." After the descent of the Holy Spirit at Pentecost, St. Peter stood up to preach the first Christian sermon. He told those who listened to him that they had crucified the Messiah but that God had raised him from the dead. When they were moved by his preaching and asked what they should do, his answer was the same, "Repent, and be baptized." Neither our Lord, nor St. John the Baptist, nor St. Peter required holiness before they would accept souls into the kingdom. That would come later. The gateway to the kingdom is repentance.

As the author of the Epistle to the Hebrews tells us, repentance is the foundation of the Christian life. But he urges that we should not be content to remain at this beginning. We should "go on unto perfection." In baptism, we are made partakers of the death of Christ. It is interesting to note that in the Russian language, the word for baptism is not derived, as our English word is, from the Greek. The Russian word is derived from the word for cross. The Christians of the Russian Church, by the very name they use for this sacrament of birth into the family of God, recognize that what happens at baptism is a sharing in what happened at the cross. By baptism, we share in the death of Christ.

Crucifixion was not a quick death. A man who was crucified took a long time to die. But he had died to this earthly life even though the life still lingered in him as he hung on the cross. He would never return to it. He would never again resume the old life. He had died to it, left it forever; but he still had to endure, often for many long and sorrowful hours, the pains of the dying process. This is a picture of what is involved in the Christian life. St. Paul reminds us that, as Christians, we are crucified with Christ. We are crucified men, dead to the old life of the world, and yet still having to experience the continuing process of dying to it. Repentance brings us back into union with him, but we must go on from there until the process is complete.

There is an old legend that the seed of the forbidden tree was transmitted on down the centuries, until from the same wood were cut the timbers for the cross. This is of course no more than a typical medieval conceit, but it enshrines a profound truth. God took the very instrument of our destruction and turned it into the means of our deliverance. As dying, and behold we live. We see a foreshadowing of this in the incident of the brazen serpent in the Old Testament. The children of Israel had been bitten by serpents in the desert. Moses made a serpent of brass and put it on a pole. As many as looked on it were cured of their hurt. The very thing that caused their sickness was used as the means of their healing. Our Lord was aware of this parallel to his own work. "As Moses lifted up the serpent in the wilderness," he said, "even so must the Son of Man be lifted up; that whosoever believeth in him should not perish, but have everlasting life." Not all men perceive that the cure for their sickness is here. They look at the cross and see there only pain and death. But this death is life-giving, and this pain is for our healing.

St. Thomas à Kempis remarked: "Repentance begins to reveal to us many good things to which dissipation had blinded us." This is to speak of the same truth in a different way. Repentance begins to restore clear vision to us. The way of Christ, which looked like the way of death, is perceived to be in fact the way to life; while the way of our past sins which had seemed a way to life is seen to have been leading in the opposite direction. The deceiving mirages and dark fantasies begin to fade, and our faces are set toward the light and the sun. Sin is only death pretending to be life. When we repent, we begin to see that this is true.

With the new understanding resulting from repentance and with the power and encouragement that God's forgiveness brings, it is for us to go on from that beginning toward true holiness of life which our Lord requires from those who follow him ("Be ye holy, as I am holy"). The great difference between a man and an animal or a vegetable is that a man doesn't have to stay the way he is. He can take a look at himself and change himself. This is a unique ability. A horse cannot do it, nor can a cabbage. But a man can. A man can deliberately take steps to alter things about himself. He can decide to do exercises for his biceps and, if he is determined enough, in due course a change in them will appear. He can decide to acquire knowledge about some subject and, within the limitations of his intellect, he will presently know a good deal more about it than he did before. The life of the spirit is no exception. The struggle against temptation begins always in the mind. It is here that the victory over all sins is ultimately won or lost. So it is by what is commonly called "mental prayer" that the soul may best hope to grow stronger.

Many people scarcely know what is meant by "meditation." They connect it vaguely with something like sitting in a garden chair in the cool of the evening and having pleasant uplifting thoughts about nothing in particular. This is daydreaming, not meditation. A meditation is a fairly exact spiritual exercise deliberately aimed at building up the soul, just as different kinds of calisthenics are designed to build up various parts of the body.

There are different methods of making a meditation. They are known by the names of the spiritual giants who developed them and wrote them down for later souls to use. There are the "Ignation method" (St. Ignatius Loyola), the "Salesian" (St. Francis de Sales), and the methods of St. Peter of Alcantara, and others. Books are available which describe in detail these different ways of meditating, and there is neither room nor need to go into them here. But, in order to encourage people who perhaps have never seriously considered this kind of prayer to start to use it, we will take a brief look at a very simple and easy method, and see what it involves.

This method of meditation has three stages. After a moment of recollection to fix the mind on what we are about to do, and a prayer that God may help us to do it, we can begin. The first stage is "adoration" (*Jesus before the eyes*). We take some incident in the Gospel story and quite simply look at our Lord in it. A picture may help, but most people's imagination is good enough for them to dwell on the scene without any external assistance of that kind. Any incident may be chosen. For an example, let us think of our Lord being nailed to the cross. We look at the scene. How brave he is, how calm, how full of love, how free from self-pity or bitterness against those responsible. We look at him there. We watch him. We admire him, we adore him. The first stage of the meditation consists in just doing this for as long as we wish. The time taken for this part of the exercise will vary from one person to another, but should be approximately one third of the total time available.

The second stage develops very easily and naturally from the first. It is called "communion" (*Jesus in the heart*). While still looking at Jesus and admiring and loving him in the scene before us, we now begin to draw into ourselves the virtues we have seen in him. "O Lord, I would be brave like you, calm and full of love. Let me also be free from self-pity and from feelings of bitterness against others. Come to me with your courage and your love for men. Let me be like you. Come to my heart, Lord Jesus, and fill it with your love and your courage."

The third stage is called "co-operation" (*Jesus in the hands*). The purpose of a meditation is that we should grow in grace. Prayer must issue out into action. In this last stage, the will is brought into play. We have looked at our Lord in this moment of his passion. We have loved him and admired him for the qualities of character which we have seen in him there. We have tried to draw them, and him, into our hearts. In this third stage, we now resolve to show these qualities ourselves when the occasion calls for them in the future. "Lord, I will be brave like you. I will be calm and free of self-pity. I resolve to feel no bitterness either the next time someone injures me. Be with me, Lord, and strengthen my will and my resolution to copy your example in this way in the future."

So our simple three-stage meditation comes to an end. It can be based on any Gospel incident we like to choose; and the same incident can be used again and again. What this spiritual exercise causes us to do is to look at Christ and to love him. Whatever people admire has an influence upon them. They consciously or unconsciously mold themselves upon it. A meditation is designed to help us to look at and to admire the Lord Jesus Christ and to allow that admiration to work its effect upon us.

We have seen that the battle against sin is won or lost first in the mind and only after that does the corresponding action follow. By means of a meditation like the one outlined above, it is sometimes possible to fight a battle before it arrives. We may know that we are going to be obliged to enter into an occasion of temptation during the course of the day. Before the day begins, a meditation can be made leading up to the particular virtue of which we shall stand especially in need before the day is done. Perhaps you know that in the afternoon you are going to have to meet with someone who is inclined to exasperate and irritate you. You are going to need to call up your reserves of patience and kindliness if you are to avoid an angry scene with him. A meditation made the previous evening, or before the day begins, based on our Lord's patient dealing with the crowds who thronged him, even when he was worn out at the end of a long day, may help to reinforce your will and give you the patience you need to show something of that same quality to your tiresome friend. You may be able to come fore-armed to the battle, and so beat down the temptation to ill-temper when it comes.

Each of us can use the Gospel incidents that appeal most readily to us, but a brief indication may be helpful to show how a meditation could be made as a defense against each of the seven root sins:

Against pride: The manger scene: The son of God, the Lord of heaven and earth humbled himself to be born in a stable and laid in a manger.

Against envy: Jesus in the house of the rich man, Simon: he accepts the hospitality offered to him quite simply and naturally, neither overawed by wealth nor resentful of it.

Against anger: Before the Sanhedrin: They rail at him, insult him and spit on him, but he remains completely calm and self-possessed.

Against sloth: The carpenter's shop in Nazareth: Joseph labored there, and for thirty years, our Lord was "subject unto him" and worked as a carpenter's helper.

Against covetousness: Our Lord on the road, walking with his disciples from one village to another: His simple clothing was apparently all he ever owned.

Against gluttony: The marriage at Cana of Galilee: He enjoyed a happy social occasion but never forgot who he was.

Against lust: The woman taken in adultery: Her accusers gloat over the prurient detail that she was taken in the very act. Jesus brings their own sin home to them and then deals firmly but gently with the woman herself.

There is a story told about St. Jerome, the great scholar of the early Church. It was drawing near to Christmas, and St. Jerome was making preparation for the proper keeping of the festival. One night, in a dream, the Christ Child appeared to him. "What present are you planning to give me on my birthday, Jerome?" he asked. St. Jerome thought of his great works of theology. But they were not what our Lord wanted. He already knew a great deal more about God than Jerome did. Should he offer his life of asceticism, his vigils, and fastings? These were acceptable, certainly, but it seemed that they were not exactly what the Holy Child was hoping for. The dream faded and Jerome awoke. "I will offer him my sins," he said. And so, before Christmas, Jerome made solemn repentance for his sins and gave to our Saviour the thing that above all he wants to receive and take away from us. There is joy in the presence of the angels of God over one sinner that repenteth.

It is significant how often the prefix "re" appears in the words we use when we are talking of God's work for men: religion, redemption, restoration, reconciliation, repentance, resurrection. The rhythm of nature speaks of the same thing. We see the cycle of birth, life, death, and resurrection as nature passes through the successive seasons of the year. In the world of the spirit, there is a parallel cycle: sin—separation—repentance—reconciliation. Both cycles depend on God and neither therefore will ever fail. "While the earth remaineth, seedtime and harvest, and cold and heat, and summer and winter, and day and night shall not cease." Neither shall fail the everlasting mercy of God reaching out in immediate love and forgiveness to his children when they repent and return to him.

PRAYERS

Almighty and everlasting God, who hatest nothing that thou hast made, and dost forgive the sins of all them that are penitent: Create and make in us new and contrite hearts, that we worthily lamenting our sins, and acknowledging our wretchedness, may obtain of thee, the God of all mercy, perfect remission and forgiveness; through Jesus Christ our Lord. Amen.

O Lord, we beseech thee mercifully hear our prayers, and spare all those who confess their sins unto thee; that they, whose consciences by sin are accused, by thy merciful pardon may be absolved, through Jesus Christ our Lord. Amen.

Almighty Father, who of thy great love to men didst give thy dearly beloved Son to die for us. Grant that through his Cross our sins may be put away, and remember no more against us;

and that, cleansed by his blood, and mindful of his sufferings, we may take up our cross daily and follow him in newness of life, until we come to his everlasting kingdom; through the same thy Son, Jesus Christ our Lord. Amen.

SCRIPTURE

God so loved the world, that he gave his only begotten Son, that whosoever believeth in him should not perish, but have eternal life.

John 3:16

If we say that we have no sin, we deceive ourselves, and the truth is not in us. But, if we confess our sins, he is faithful and just to forgive us our sins, and to cleanse us from all unrighteousness.

I John 1:8-9

Then said he, Lo, I come to do thy will, O God. . . . By the which will, we are sanctified through the offering of the body of Jesus Christ once for all. And every priest standeth daily ministering and offering oftentimes the same sacrifices, which can never take away sins. But this man, after he had offered one sacrifice for sins for ever, sat down on the right hand of God. For by one offering he hath perfected for ever them that are sanctified.

Hebrews 10:9, 10-14

Format by Barbara Luttringhaus
Set in Linotype Old Style Number 1
Composed, printed and bound by The Haddon Craftsmen, Inc.
HARPER & ROW, PUBLISHERS, INCORPORATED